Data Lake Development with Big Data

Explore architectural approaches to building Data Lakes that ingest, index, manage, and analyze massive amounts of data using Big Data technologies

Pradeep Pasupuleti

Beulah Salome Purra

BIRMINGHAM - MUMBAI

Data Lake Development with Big Data

First published: November 2015

Production reference: 1241115

Published by Packt Publishing Ltd.
Livery Place
35 Livery Street
Birmingham B3 2PB, UK.

ISBN 978-1-78588-808-3

www.packtpub.com

Credits

Authors

Pradeep Pasupuleti

Beulah Salome Purra

Reviewer

Dr. Kornel Amadeusz
Skałkowski

Commissioning Editor

Priya Singh

Acquisition Editor

Ruchita Bhansali

Content Development Editor

Rohit Kumar Singh

Technical Editor

Saurabh Malhotra

Copy Editor

Trishya Hajare

Project Coordinator

Izzat Contractor

Proofreader

Safis Editing

Indexer

Hemangini Bari

Graphics

Jason Monteiro

Kirk D'Penha

Production Coordinator

Shantanu N. Zagade

Cover Work

Shantanu N. Zagade

About the Authors

Pradeep Pasupuleti has 18 years of experience in architecting and developing distributed and real-time data-driven systems. He constantly explores ways to use the power and promise of advanced analytics-driven platforms to solve the problems of the common man. He founded Datatma, a consulting firm, with a mission to humanize Big Data analytics, putting it to use to solve simple problems that serve a higher purpose.

He architected robust Big Data-enabled automated learning engines that enterprises regularly use in production in order to save time, money, and the lives of humans.

He built solid interdisciplinary data science teams that bridged the gap between theory and practice, thus, creating compelling data products. His primary focus is always to ensure his customers are delighted by assisting and addressing their business problems through data products that use Big Data technologies and algorithms. He consistently demonstrated thought leadership by solving high-dimensional data problems and getting phenomenal results.

He has performed strategic leadership roles in technology consulting, advising Fortune 100 companies on Big Data strategy and creating Big Data Centers of Excellence.

He has worked on use cases such as enterprise Data Lake, fraud detection, patient re-admission prediction, student performance prediction, claims optimization sentiment mining, cloud infrastructure SLA violation prediction, data leakage prevention, and mainframe offloaded ETL on Hadoop.

In the book *Pig Design Patterns*, *Packt Publishing*, he has compiled his learning and experiences from the challenges involved in building Hadoop-driven data products such as data ingest, data cleaning and validating, data transformation, dimensionality reduction, and many other interesting Big Data war stories.

Out of his office hours, he enjoys running marathons, exploring archeological sites, finding patterns in unrelated data sources, mentoring start-ups, and budding researchers.

He can be reached at `Pasupuleti.pradeepkumar@gmail.com` and `https://in.linkedin.com/in/pradeeppasupuleti`.

Acknowledgement

This book is dedicated to the loving memory of my mother, Smt. Sumathy; without her never-failing encouragement and everlasting love I would have never been half as good.

First and foremost, I have to thank my father, Sri. Prabhakar Pasupuleti, who never ceases to be a constant source of inspiration, a ray of hope, humility and strength, and whose support and guidance have given me the courage to chase my dreams.

I should also express my deep sense of gratitude to each of my family members, Sushma, Sresht, and Samvruth, who stood by me at every moment through very tough times and enabled me to complete this book.

I would like to sincerely thank all my teachers who were instrumental in shaping me. Among them, I would like to thank Usha Madam, Vittal Rao Sir, Gopal Krishna Sir, and Brindavan Sir for their stellar role in improving me.

I would also like to thank all my friends for their understanding in many ways. Their friendship makes my life a wonderful experience. I cannot list all the names here, but you are always on my mind.

Special thanks to the team at Packt for their contribution to this book.

Finally, I would like to thank my team, Salome et.al, that has placed immense faith in the power of Big Data analytics and built cutting edge data products.

Thank you lord, for always being there for me.

Beulah Salome Purra has over 11 years of experience and she specializes in building highly scalable distributed systems. She has worked extensively on architecting multiple large-scale Big Data solutions for Fortune 100 companies. Her core expertise lies in working on Big Data Analytics. In her current role at ATMECS, her focus is on building robust and scalable data products that extract value from huge data assets.

She can be reached at `https://www.linkedin.com/in/beulahsalomep`.

I am grateful to my parents, Rathnam and Padma, who have constantly encouraged and supported me throughout. I would like to thank my husband, Pratap, for his help on this book, his patience, love, and support; my brothers, Joel and Michael, for all their support.

I would like to profusely thank Pradeep Pasupuleti for mentoring me; working with him has been an enriching experience. I can't thank him enough for his constant encouragement, guidance, support, and for providing me an opportunity to work with him on this book.

Special thanks to David Hawke, Sanjay Singh, and Ravi Velagapudi—the leadership team at ATMECS—for their encouragement and support while I was writing this book.

Thanks to the editors and reviewers at Packt for all their effort in making this book better.

About the Reviewer

Dr. Kornel Amadeusz Skałkowski has a solid academic and industrial background. For more than 5 years, he worked as an assistant at AGH University of Science and Technology in Krakow. In 2015, he obtained his PhD. in the subject of machine learning-based adaptation of the SOA systems. He has cooperated with several companies on various projects concerning intelligent systems, machine learning, and Big Data. Currently, he works as a Big Data developer for SAP SE.

He is the co-author of 19 papers concerning software engineering, SOA systems, and machine learning. He also works as a reviewer for the American Journal of Software Engineering and Applications. He has participated in numerous European and national scientific projects. His research interests include machine learning, Big Data, and software engineering.

I would like to kindly thank my family, relatives, and friends, for their endless patience and support during the reviewing of this book.

www.PacktPub.com

Support files, eBooks, discount offers, and more

For support files and downloads related to your book, please visit www.PacktPub.com.

Did you know that Packt offers eBook versions of every book published, with PDF and ePub files available? You can upgrade to the eBook version at www.PacktPub.com and as a print book customer, you are entitled to a discount on the eBook copy. Get in touch with us at service@packtpub.com for more details.

At www.PacktPub.com, you can also read a collection of free technical articles, sign up for a range of free newsletters and receive exclusive discounts and offers on Packt books and eBooks.

https://www2.packtpub.com/books/subscription/packtlib

Do you need instant solutions to your IT questions? PacktLib is Packt's online digital book library. Here, you can search, access, and read Packt's entire library of books.

Why subscribe?

- Fully searchable across every book published by Packt
- Copy and paste, print, and bookmark content
- On demand and accessible via a web browser

Free access for Packt account holders

If you have an account with Packt at www.PacktPub.com, you can use this to access PacktLib today and view 9 entirely free books. Simply use your login credentials for immediate access.

Table of Contents

Preface

The book *Data Lake Development with Big Data* is a practical guide to help you learn the essential architectural approaches to design and build Data Lakes. It walks you through the various components of Data Lakes, such as data intake, management, consumption, and governance with a specific focus on practical implementation scenarios.

Data Lake is a highly scalable data platform for better search, analytical processing, and cheaper storage of huge volumes of any structured data acquired from disparate sources.

Traditional Data Management systems are constrained by data silos, upfront data modeling, rigid data structures, and schema-based write approaches while storing and processing data. This hampers the holistic analysis of data residing in multiple silos and excludes unstructured data sources from analysis. The data is generally modeled to answer known business questions.

With Data Lake, there are no more data silos; all the data can be utilized to get a coherent view that can power a new generation of data-aware analytics applications. With Data Lake, you don't have to know all the business questions in advance, as the data can be modeled later using the schema-less approach and it is possible to ask complex far-reaching questions on all the data at any time to find out hidden patterns and complex relationships in the data.

After reading this book, you will be able to address the shortcoming of traditional data systems through the best practices highlighted in this book for building Data Lake. You will understand the complete lifecycle of architecting/building Data Lake with Big Data technologies such as Hadoop, Storm, Spark, and Splunk. You will gain a comprehensive knowledge of various stages in Data Lake such as data intake, data management, and data consumption with focus on the practical use cases at each stage. You will benefit from the book's detailed coverage of data governance, data security, data lineage tracking, metadata management, data provisioning, and consumption.

As Data Lake is such an advanced complex topic, we are honored and excited to author the first book of its kind in the world. However, at the same time, as the topic being so vast and as there is no one-size-fits-all kind of Data Lake architecture, it is very challenging to appeal to a wide audience footprint. As it is a mini series book, which limits the page count, it is extremely difficult to cover every topic in detail without breaking the ceiling. Given these constraints, we have taken a reader-centric approach in writing this book because the broader understanding of the overall concept of Data Lake is far more important than the in-depth understanding of all the technologies and architectural possibilities that go into building Data Lake.

Using this guiding principle, we refrained from the in-depth coverage of any single topic, because we could not possibly do justice to it. At the same time we made efforts to organize chapters to mimic the sequential flow of data in a typical organization so that it is intuitive for the reader to quickly grasp the concepts of Data Lake from an organizational data flow perspective. In order to make the abstract concepts relatable to the real world, we have followed a use case-based approach where practical implementation scenarios of each key Data Lake component are explained. This we believe will help the reader quickly understand the architectural implications of various Big Data technologies that are used for building these components.

What this book covers

Chapter 1, The Need for Data Lake, helps you understand what Data Lake is, its architecture and key components, and the business contexts where Data Lake can be successfully deployed. You will also learn the limitations of the traditional data architectures and how Data Lake addresses some of these inadequacies and provides significant benefits.

Chapter 2, Data Intake, helps you understand the Intake Tier in detail where we will explore the process of obtaining huge volumes of data into Data Lake. You will learn the technology perspective of the various External Data Sources and Hadoop-based data transfer mechanisms to pull or push data into Data Lake.

Chapter 3, Data Integration, Quality, and Enrichment, explores the processes that are performed on vast quantities of data in the Management Tier. You will get a deeper understanding of the key technology aspects and components such as profiling, validation, integration, cleansing, standardization, and enrichment using Hadoop ecosystem components.

Chapter 4, Data Discovery and Consumption, helps you understand how data can be discovered, packaged, and provisioned, for it to be consumed by the downstream systems. You will learn the key technology aspects, architectural guidance and tools for data discovery, and data provisioning functionalities.

Chapter 5, Data Governance, explores the details, need, and utility of data governance in a Data Lake environment. You will learn how to deal with metadata management, lineage tracking, data lifecycle management to govern the usability, security, integrity, and availability of the data through the data governance processes applied on the data in Data Lake. This chapter also explores how the current Data Lake can evolve in a futuristic setting.

What you need for this book

As this book covers only the architectural details and acts as a guide for decision-making, we have not provided any code examples. Hence, there is no explicit software prerequisite.

Who this book is for

Data Lake Development with Big Data is intended for architects and senior managers who are responsible for building a strategy around their current data architecture, helping them identify the need for Data Lake implementation in an organizational business context.

Good knowledge on master data management, information lifecycle management, data governance, data product design, data engineering, systems architecture, and experience on Big Data technologies such as Hadoop, Spark, Splunk, and Storm is necessary.

Conventions

In this book, you will find a number of text styles that distinguish between different kinds of information. Here are some examples of these styles and an explanation of their meaning.

Code words in text, database table names, folder names, filenames, file extensions, pathnames, dummy URLs, user input, and Twitter handles are shown as follows: "We can include other contexts through the use of the `include` directive."

New terms and **important words** are shown in bold. Words that you see on the screen, for example, in menus or dialog boxes, appear in the text like this: "Clicking the **Next** button moves you to the next screen."

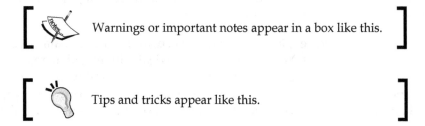

> Warnings or important notes appear in a box like this.

> Tips and tricks appear like this.

Reader feedback

Feedback from our readers is always welcome. Let us know what you think about this book—what you liked or disliked. Reader feedback is important for us as it helps us develop titles that you will really get the most out of.

To send us general feedback, simply e-mail `feedback@packtpub.com`, and mention the book's title in the subject of your message.

If there is a topic that you have expertise in and you are interested in either writing or contributing to a book, see our author guide at `www.packtpub.com/authors`.

Customer support

Now that you are the proud owner of a Packt book, we have a number of things to help you to get the most from your purchase.

Errata

Although we have taken every care to ensure the accuracy of our content, mistakes do happen. If you find a mistake in one of our books—maybe a mistake in the text or the code—we would be grateful if you could report this to us. By doing so, you can save other readers from frustration and help us improve subsequent versions of this book. If you find any errata, please report them by visiting http://www.packtpub.com/submit-errata, selecting your book, clicking on the **Errata Submission Form** link, and entering the details of your errata. Once your errata are verified, your submission will be accepted and the errata will be uploaded to our website or added to any list of existing errata under the Errata section of that title.

To view the previously submitted errata, go to https://www.packtpub.com/books/content/support and enter the name of the book in the search field. The required information will appear under the **Errata** section.

Piracy

Piracy of copyrighted material on the Internet is an ongoing problem across all media. At Packt, we take the protection of our copyright and licenses very seriously. If you come across any illegal copies of our works in any form on the Internet, please provide us with the location address or website name immediately so that we can pursue a remedy.

Please contact us at copyright@packtpub.com with a link to the suspected pirated material.

We appreciate your help in protecting our authors and our ability to bring you valuable content.

Questions

If you have a problem with any aspect of this book, you can contact us at questions@packtpub.com, and we will do our best to address the problem.

1
The Need for Data Lake

In this chapter, we will understand the rationale behind building a Data Lake in an organization that has huge data assets. The following topics will be covered in this chapter:

- Explore the emerging need for Data Lake by understanding the limitations of the traditional architectures
- Decipher how a Data Lake addresses the inadequacies of traditional architectures and provides significant benefits in terms of time and cost
- Understand what a Data Lake is and also its architecture
- Practical guidance on the key points to consider before deciding to build a Data Lake
- Understand the key components that could be a part of a Data Lake and comprehend how crucial each of these components are to build a successful Data Lake

Before the Data Lake

In this section, let us quickly look at how the Data Lake has evolved from a historical perspective.

From the time data-intensive applications were used to solve business problems, we have seen many evolutionary steps in the way data has been stored, managed, analyzed, and visualized.

The earlier systems were designed to answer questions about the past; questions such as *what were my total sales in the last year?*, were answered by machines built around monolithic processors that ran COBOL, accessing data from tapes and disks. Since the dawn of faster processors and better storage, businesses were able to slice and dice data to find fine-grained answers from subsets of data; these questions resembled: *what was the sales performance of x unit in y geography in z timeframe?*

If we extract one common pattern, all the earlier systems were developed for business users, in order to help them make decisions for their businesses. The current breed of data systems empowers people like you and me to make decisions and improve the way we live. This is an ultimate paradigm shift brought by the advances in myriad technologies.

For many of us, the technologies that run in the background are transparent, while we consult applications that help us make decisions that alter our immediate future profoundly. We use applications to help us navigate to an address (mapping), decide on our holidays (weather and holiday planning sites), get a summary of product reviews (review sites), get similar products (recommendation engines), connect and grow professionally (professional social networks), and the list goes on.

All these applications use enabling technologies that understand natural languages, process humungous amounts of data, store and effortlessly process our personal data such as images and audio, and even extract intelligence from them by tagging our faces and finding relationships. Each of us, in a way, contributes to the flooding of these application servers with our personal data in the form of our preferences, likes, affiliations, networks, hobbies, friends, images, and videos.

If we can attribute one fundamental cause for today's explosion of data, it should be the proliferation of ubiquitous internet connectivity and the Smartphone; with it comes the exponential number of applications that transmit and store a variety of data.

Juxtaposing the growth of Smartphones and the internet with the rapid decline of storage costs and cloud computing, which also bring down the processing costs, we can immediately comprehend that the traditional data architectures do not scale to handle the volume and variety of data; thus cannot, answer questions that you and I want. They work well, extremely well for business users, but not directly for us.

In order to democratize the value hidden in data and thus empower common customers to use data for day-to-day decision making, organizations should first store and extract value from the different types of data being collected in such a huge quantities. For all this to happen, the following two key developments have had a revolutionary impact:

- The development of distributed computing architectures that can scale linearly and perform computations at an unbelievable pace

- The development of new-age algorithms that can analyze natural languages, comprehend the semantics of the spoken words and special types, run Neural Nets, perform deep learning, graph social network interactions, perform constraint-based stochastic optimization, and so on

Earlier systems were simply not architected to scale linearly and store/analyze these many types of data. They are good for the purpose they were initially built for. They excelled as a historical data store that can offload structured data from **Online Transaction Processing (OLTP)** systems, perform transformations, cleanse it, slice-dice and summarize it, and then feed it to **Online Analytical Processing (OLAP)** systems. Business Intelligence tools consume the exhaust of the OLAP systems and spew good-looking reports religiously at regular intervals so that the business users can make the decisions.

We can immediately grasp the glaring differences between the earlier systems and the new age systems by looking at these major aspects:

- The storage and processing differs in the way it scales (distributed versus monolithic)

- In earlier systems, data is managed in relational systems versus NoSQL, MPP, and CEP systems in the new age Big Data systems

- Traditional systems cannot handle high-velocity data that is efficiently ingested and processed by Big Data applications

- Structured data is predominantly used in earlier systems versus unstructured data being used in Big Data systems along with structured data

- Traditional systems have limitations around the scale of data that they can handle; Big Data systems are scalable and can handle humongous amounts of data

- Traditional analytic algorithms such as linear/logistic regressions versus cutting edge algorithms such as random forests-ensemble methods, stochastic optimizations, deep learning, and NLP being regularly used in Big Data systems

- Reports and drilldowns are the mainstay, versus the advanced visualizations such as Tag cloud and Heat map, which are some of the choicest reporting advances in the Big Data era

Data Lake is one such architecture that has evolved to address the need of the organizations to adapt to the new business reality. Organizations today listen to the customer's voice more than ever; they are sensitive to customer feedback and negative remarks—it hurts their bottom line if they don't. Organizations understand their customers more intimately than ever before—they know your every move, literally, through behavioral profiling. Finally, organizations use all the data at their disposal to help customers leverage it for their personal benefit. In order to catch up with the changing business landscape, there is immense potential for building a Data Lake to store, process, and analyze huge amounts of structured and unstructured data.

The following figure elucidates the vital differences between traditional and Big Data systems:

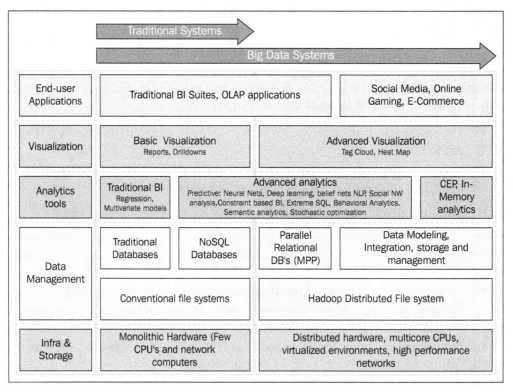

Traditional versus Big Data systems

Need for Data Lake

Now that we have glimpsed the past and understood how various systems evolved in time, let us explore in this section, a few important reasons why Data Lakes have evolved and what problems they try to address. Let's start with a contextual overview.

One of the key driving forces behind the onslaught of Big Data is the rapid spread of unstructured data (which constitutes 90 percent of the data). The increase in mobile phones, wider internet coverage, faster data networks, cheaper cloud storage, and falling compute/storage prices, all contribute to the spurt of Big Data in recent years. A few studies reveal that we produce as much data every 15 minutes, as was created from the beginning of the time, to the year 2003. This roughly coincides with the mobility/cloud usage proliferation.

Big data is not only about massive data capture and storage at a cheaper price point, but the real value of storing Big Data comes from intelligently combining the historical data that already exists inside an organization with the unstructured data. This helps in gaining new and better insights that improve business performance.

For example, in retail, it could imply better and rapid services to customers; in R&D, it could imply performing iterative tests over much larger samples in a faster way; in healthcare, it could imply quicker and more precise diagnoses of illnesses.

For an organization to be really successful to reap the latent benefits of Big Data, it needs two basic capabilities:

- Technology should be in place to enable organizations to acquire, store, combine, and enrich huge volumes of unstructured and structured data in raw format
- Ability to perform analytics, real-time and near-real-time analysis at scale, on these huge volumes in an iterative way

To address the preceding two business needs, the concept of Data Lake has become one of the empowering data captures and processing capabilities for Big Data analytics.

The Data Lake makes it possible to store all the data, ask complex and radically bigger business questions, and find out hidden patterns and relationships from the data.

Using a traditional system, an enterprise may not have the solution to find out whether there is any hidden value in the data that the enterprise is not storing right now or letting go as waste. We don't really know what hidden value this data contains at the time of data acquisition. We might know a miniscule percentage of questions to ask at the data acquisition time, but we can never know what questions could materialize at a later point of time. Essentially, a Data Lake tries to address this core business problem.

While reasons abound to explain the need of a Data Lake, one of the core reasons is the dramatic decrease of storage costs and thus enabling organizations to store humungous amounts of data.

Let us look at a few reasons for the emergence of the Data Lake with reference to the aspects in which the traditional approaches fail:

- The traditional **data warehouse (DW)** systems are not designed to integrate, scale, and handle this exponential growth of multi-structured data. With the emergence of Big Data, there is a need to bring together data from disparate sources and to generate a meaning out of it; new types of data ranging from social text, audio, video, sensors, and clickstream data have to be integrated to find out complex relationships in the data.

- The traditional systems lack the ability to integrate data from disparate sources. This leads to proliferation of data silos, due to which, business users view data in various perspectives, which eventually thwarts them from making precise and appropriate decisions.

- The schema-on-write approach followed by traditional systems mandate the data model and analytical framework to be designed before any data is loaded. Upfront data modeling fails in a Big Data scenario as we are unaware of the nature of incoming data and the exploratory analysis that has to be performed in order to gain hidden insights. Analytical frameworks are designed to answer only specific questions identified at the design time. This approach does not allow for data discovery.

- With traditional approaches, optimization for analytics is time consuming and incurs huge costs. Such optimization enables known analytics, but fails when there are new requirements.

- In traditional systems, it is difficult to identify what data is available and to integrate the data to answer a question. Metadata management and lineage tracking of data is not available or difficult to implement; manual recreation of data lineage is error-prone and consumes a lot of time.

Defining Data Lake

In the preceding sections, we had a quick overview of how the traditional systems evolved over time and understood their shortcomings with respect to the newer forms of data. In this section, let us discover what a Data Lake is and how it addresses the gaps masquerading as opportunities.

A Data Lake has flexible definitions. At its core, it is a data storage and processing repository in which all of the data in an organization can be placed so that every internal and external systems', partners', and collaborators' data flows into it and insights spring out.

The following list details out in a nutshell what a Data Lake is:

- Data Lake is a huge repository that holds every kind of data in its raw format until it is needed by anyone in the organization to analyze.

- Data Lake is not Hadoop. It uses different tools. Hadoop only implements a subset of functionalities.

- Data Lake is not a database in the traditional sense of the word. A typical implementation of Data Lake uses various NoSQL and In-Memory databases that could co-exist with its relational counterparts.

- A Data Lake cannot be implemented in isolation. It has to be implemented alongside a data warehouse as it complements various functionalities of a DW.

- It stores large volumes of both unstructured and structured data. It also stores fast-moving streamed data from machine sensors and logs.

- It advocates a Store-All approach to huge volumes of data.

- It is optimized for data crunching with a high-latency batch mode and it is not geared for transaction processing.

- It helps in creating data models that are flexible and could be revised without database redesign.

- It can quickly perform data enrichment that helps in achieving data enhancement, augmentation, classification, and standardization of the data.

- All of the data stored in the Data Lake can be utilized to get an all-inclusive view. This enables near-real-time, more precise predictive models that go beyond sampling and aid in generating multi-dimensional models too.

- It is a data scientist's favorite hunting ground. He gets to access the data stored in its raw glory at its most granular level, so that he can perform any ad-hoc queries, and build an advanced model at any time—*Iteratively*. The classic data warehouse approach does not support this ability to condense the time between data intake and insight generation.

- It enables to model the data, not only in the traditional relational way, but the real value from the data can emanate from modeling it in the following ways:

  - As a graph to find the interactions between elements; for example, Neo4J
  - As a document store to cluster similar text; for example, MongoDB
  - As a columnar store for fast updates and search; for example, HBase
  - As a key-value store for lightning the fast search; for example, Riak

A key attribute of a Data Lake is that data is not classified when it is stored. As a result, the data preparation, cleansing, and transformation tasks are eliminated; these tasks generally take a lion's share of time in a Data Warehouse. Storing data in its rawest form enables us to find answers from the data for which we do not know the questions yet; whereas a traditional data warehouse is optimized for answering questions that we already know—thus preparation of the data is a mandatory step here.

This reliance on raw data makes it easy for the business to consume just what it wants from the lake and refine it for the purpose. Crucially, in the Data Lake, the raw data makes multiple perspectives possible on the same source so that everyone can get their own viewpoints on the data, in a manner that enables their local business's success.

This flexibility of storing all data in a single Big Data repository and creating multiple viewpoints require that the Data Lake implements controls for corporate data consistency. To achieve this, targeted information governance policies are enforced. Using **Master Data Management (MDM)**, **Research Data Management (RDM)**, and other security controls, corporate collaboration and access controls are implemented.

Key benefits of Data Lake

Having understood the need for the Data Lake and the business/technology context of its evolution, let us now summarize the important benefits in the following list:

- **Scale as much as you can**: Theoretically, the HDFS-based storage of Hadoop gives you the flexibility to support arbitrarily large clusters while maintaining a constant price per performance curve even as it scales. This means, your data storage can be scaled horizontally to cater to any need at a judicious cost. To gain more space, all you have to do is plug in a new cluster and then Hadoop scales seamlessly. Hadoop brings you the incredible facility to run the code close to storage, allowing quicker processing of massive data sets. The usage of Hadoop for underlying storage makes the Data Lake more scalable at a better price point than Data Warehouses by an order of magnitude. This allows for the retention of huge amounts of data.

- **Plug in disparate data sources**: Unlike a data warehouse that can only ingest structured data, a Hadoop-powered Data Lake has an inherent ability to ingest multi-structured and massive datasets from disparate sources. This means that the Data Lake can store literally any type of data such as multimedia, binary, XML, logs, sensor data, social chatter, and so on. This is one huge benefit that removes data silos and enables quick integration of datasets.

- **Acquire high-velocity data**: In order to efficiently stream high-speed data in huge volumes, the Data Lake makes use of tools that can acquire and queue it. The Data Lake utilizes tools such as Kafka, Flume, Scribe, and Chukwa to acquire high-velocity data. This data could be the incessant social chatter in the form of Twitter feeds, WhatsApp messages, or it could be sensor data from the machine exhaust. This ability to acquire high-velocity data and integrate with large volumes of historical data gives Data Lake the edge over Data Warehousing systems, which could not do any of these as effectively.

- **Add a structure**: To make sense of vast amounts of data stored in the Data Lake, we should create some structure around the data and pipe it into analysis applications. Applying a structure on unstructured data can be done while ingesting or after being stored in the Data Lake. A structure such as the metadata of a file, word counts, parts of speech tagging, and so on, can be created out of the unstructured data. The Data Lake gives you a unique platform where we have the ability to apply a structure on varied datasets in the same repository with a richer detail; hence, enabling you to process the combined data in advanced analytic scenarios.

- **Store in native format**: In a Data Warehouse, the data is premodeled as cubes that are the best storage structures for predetermined analysis routines at the time of ingestion. The Data Lake eliminates the need for data to be premodeled; it provides iterative and immediate access to the raw data. This enhances the delivery of analytical insights and offers unmatched flexibility to ask business questions and seek deeper answers.

- **Don't worry about schema**: Traditional data warehouses do not support the schemaless storage of data. The Data Lake leverages Hadoop's simplicity in storing data based on schemaless write and schema-based read modes. This is very helpful for data consumers to perform exploratory analysis and thus, develop new patterns from the data without worrying about its initial structure and ask far-reaching, complex questions to gain actionable intelligence.

- **Unleash your favorite SQL**: Once the data is ingested, cleansed, and stored in a structured SQL storage of the Data Lake, you can reuse the existing PL-SQL scripts. The tools such as HAWQ and IMPALA give you the flexibility to run massively parallel SQL queries while simultaneously integrating with advanced algorithm libraries such as MADLib and applications such as SAS. Performing the SQL processing inside the Data Lake decreases the time to achieving results and also consumes far less resources than performing SQL processing outside of it.

- **Advanced algorithms**: Unlike a data warehouse, the Data Lake excels at utilizing the availability of large quantities of coherent data along with deep learning algorithms to recognize items of interest that will power real-time decision analytics.

- **Administrative resources**: The Data Lake scores better than a data warehouse in reducing the administrative resources required for pulling, transforming, aggregating, and analyzing data.

Challenges in implementing a Data Lake

Having understood the key benefits of a Data Lake, we will now look at the challenges involved in implementing a Data Lake.

A Data Lake is a complex solution as there are many layers involved in building it and each layer utilizes a lot of Big Data tools and technologies to accomplish its functionality. This requires a lot of effort in terms of deployment, administration, and maintenance.

Another important aspect is data governance; as the Data Lake is aimed at bringing in all of the organization's data together, it should be built with enough governance so that it does not turn into a group of unrelated data silos.

When to go for a Data Lake implementation

In the preceding section, the top benefits of Data Lake were brought to light and we looked at how their application takes on the strategic importance in an organization.

In this section, we will try to enumerate a few key quick reference scenarios where Data Lake can be recommended as a go-to solution. Here are a few scenarios:

- Your organization is planning to extract insights from huge volumes or a high-velocity of data that a traditional data warehouse is incapable of handling.

- The business landscape is forcing your organization to adapt to market challenges by making you handle the demand for new products at a moment's notice and you have to get insights really fast.

- Your organization needs to build data products that use new data that is not yet prepared and structured. As new data becomes available, you may need to incorporate it straightaway, it probably can't wait for a schema change, building the extension and lots of delay, and it needs the insight right now.

- Your organization needs a dynamic approach in extracting insights from data where business units can tap or purify the required information when they need it.

- Your organization is looking for ways to reduce the total ownership cost of a data warehouse implementation by leveraging a Data Lake that significantly lowers storage, operational, network, and computing costs and produces better insights.

- Your organization needs to improve its topline and wants to augment internal data (such as customer data) with external data (social media and nontraditional data) from a variety of sources. This can get a broader customer view and better behavioral profile of the customer, resulting in quicker customer acquisition.

- The organization's data science/advanced analytics teams seek preserving of the original data's integrity/fidelity and need lineage tracking of data transformations to capture the origin of a specific datum and to track the lifecycle of the data as it moves through the data pipeline.

- There is a pressing need for the structuring and standardization of Big Data for new and broader data enrichment.

- There is a need for near real-time analytics for faster/better decisions and point-of-service use.

- Your organization needs an integrated data repository for plug-and-play implementation of new analytics tools and data products.

- Your data science/advanced analytics teams regularly need quick provisioning of data without having to be in an endless queue; Data Lake's capability called **Data as a Service (DaaS)** could be a solution.

Data Lake architecture

The previous sections made an effort to introduce you to the high-level concepts of the whys and whats of a Data Lake. We have now come to the last section of this chapter where you will be exposed to the internals of a Data Lake. We will take a deep dive into the architecture of Data Lake and understand the key components.

Architectural considerations

In our experience, it is practically difficult to come up with a one-size-fit-all architecture for a Data Lake. In every assignment that we have worked on earlier, we had to deal with specific tailored requirements that made us adapt the architecture to the use case.

The reason why there are multiple interpretations of the Data Lake architecture is that it totally depends on the following factors that are specific to an organization and also the business questions that the Data Lake ought to solve. To realize any of the combinations of these factors in the Data Lake, we tweaked the architecture. Here is a quick list:

- Type of data ingest (real-time ingest, micro-batch ingest, and batch ingest)
- Storage tier (raw versus structured)
- Depth of metadata collection
- Breadth of data governance
- Ability to search for data
- Structured data storage (SQL versus a variety of NoSQL databases such as graph, document, and key-value stores)
- Provisioning of data access (external versus internal)
- Speed to insights (optimized for real-time versus batch)

As you can decipher from the preceding points, there are many competing and contradictory requirements that go into building Data Lake capability. Architecting a full-blooded, production-ready Data Lake in reality takes these combinations of requirements into consideration and puts the best foot forward.

For the purpose of this book, we prefer taking a median approach for architecting a Data Lake. We believe that this approach would appeal to most of the readers who want to grasp the overarching potential of a fully blown Data Lake in the way it should be in its end state, rather than being tied down to narrow the interpretations of specific business requirements and *overfit* the architecture.

Architectural composition

For the ease of understanding, we might consider abstracting much detail and think of the Data Lake as composed of three layers and tiers.

Layers are the common functionality that cut across all the tiers. These layers are listed as follows:

- Data Governance and Security Layer
- Metadata Layer
- Information Lifecycle Management Layer

Tiers are abstractions for a similar functionality grouped together for the ease of understanding. Data flows sequentially through each tier. While the data moves from tier to tier, the layers do their bit of processing on the moving data. The following are the three tiers:

- Intake Tier
- Management Tier
- Consumption Tier

The following figure simplifies the representation of each tier in relation to the layers:

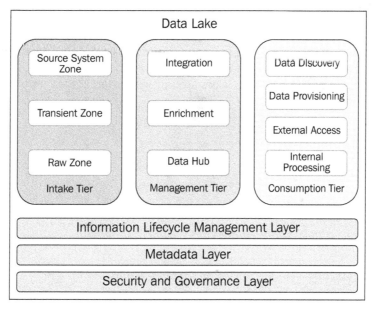

Data Lake end state architecture

Architectural details

In this section, let us go deeper and understand each of the layers and tiers of the Data Lake.

Understanding Data Lake layers

In this section, we will gain a high-level understanding of the relevance of the three horizontal layers

The Data Governance and Security Layer

The Data Governance and Security layer fixes the responsibility for governing the right data access and the rights for defining and modifying data. This layer makes sure that there is a well-documented process for the change and access control of all the data artifacts. The governance mechanism oversees methods for creation, usage, and tracking of the data lineage across various tiers of the Data Lake so that it can be combined with the security rules.

As the Data Lake stores a lot of data from various sources, the Security layer ensures that the appropriate access control and authentication provides the access to data assets on a need-to-know basis. In a practical scenario; if the data consists of both transaction and historical data, along with customer, product, and finance data, which is internally sourced, as well as from third-party sources, the security layer ensures that each subject area of the data has the applicable level of security.

This layer ensures appropriate provisioning of data with relevant security measures put in place. Hadoop's security is taken care by the inbuilt integration with Kerberos, and it is possible to ensure that the users are authenticated before they access the data or compute resources.

The following figure shows the capabilities of the Data Governance and Security layer:

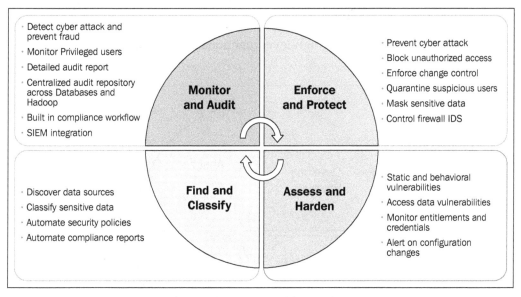

The Data Governance and Security layer

The Information Lifecycle Management layer

As the Data Lake advocates a Store-All approach to huge volumes of Big Data, it is exciting to store everything in it. The **Information Lifecycle Management (ILM)** layer ensures that there are rules governing what we can or cannot store in the Data Lake. This is because over longer periods of time, the value of data tends to decrease and the risks associated with storage increases. It does not make practical sense to fill the lake continuously, without some plan to down tier the data that has lost its use-by date; this is exactly what the ILM layer strives to achieve.

This layer primarily defines the strategy and policies for classifying which data is valuable and how long we should store a particular dataset in the Data Lake. These policies are implemented by tools that automatically purge, archive, or down tier data based on the classified policy.

The following figure depicts the high-level functionalities of the Information Lifecycle Management layer:

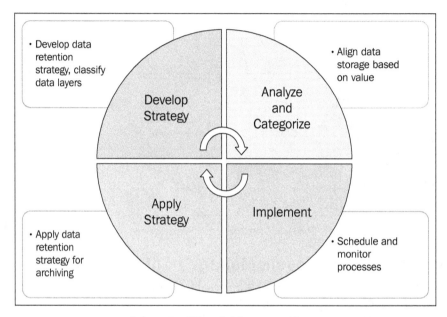

Information Lifecycle Management layer

The Metadata Layer

The Data Lake stores large quantities of structured and unstructured data and there should be a mechanism to find out the linkages between what is stored and what can be used by whom. The Metadata Layer is the heart of the Data Lake. The following list elucidates the essence of this layer:

- The Metadata layer captures vital information about the data as it enters the Data Lake and indexes this information so that users can search metadata before they access the data itself. Metadata capture is fundamental to make data more accessible and to extract value from the Data Lake.

- This layer provides vital information to the users of the Data Lake about the background and significance of the data stored in the Data Lake. For instance, data consumers could also use the metadata and find out whether a million tweets are more valued than a thousand customer records. This is accomplished by intelligently tagging every bit of data as it is ingested.

- A well-built metadata layer will allow organizations to harness the potential of the Data Lake and deliver the following mechanisms to the end users to access data and perform analytics:

    ○ **Self-Service BI (SSBI)**

    ○ **Data as a Service (DaaS)**

    ○ **Machine Learning as a Service (MLaaS)**

    ○ **Data Provisioning (DP)**

    ○ **Analytics Sandbox Provisioning (ASP)**

- The Metadata layer defines the structure for files in a Raw Zone and describes the entities inside the files. Using this base-level description, the schema evolution of the file/record is tracked by a versioning scheme. This will eventually allow you to create associations among several entities and, thereby, facilitate browsing and searching.

The following figure illustrates the various capabilities of the Metadata Layer:

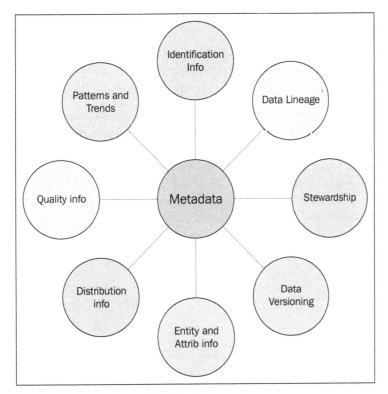

The Metadata Layer

Understanding Data Lake tiers

In the following section, let us take a short tour of each of the three tiers in the Data Lake.

The Data Intake tier

The Data Intake tier includes all the processing services that connect to external sources and the storage area for acquiring variant source data in consumable increments.

The **Intake** tier has three zones, and the data flows sequentially through these zones. The zones in the Intake tier are as follows:

- Source System Zone
- Transient landing zone
- Raw Zone

Let us examine each zone of this tier in detail:

The Source System Zone

The processing services that are needed to connect to external systems are encapsulated in the **Source System Zone**. This zone primarily deals with the connectivity and acquires data from the external source systems.

In the Source System Zone, the timeliness of data acquisition from the external sources is determined by specific application requirements. In certain classes of applications, it is required to pull log/sensor data in near-real-time and flag anomalies in real-time. In other classes of applications, it is fine to live with batch data trickling at intervals as long as a day — this class uses all the historical data to perform analysis. The Data Intake tier, therefore, should be architected in consideration to the wide latitude in storage requirements of the aforementioned application needs.

The following figure depicts the three broad types of data that would be ingested and categorized by their timeliness:

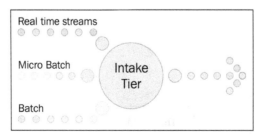

The timeliness of Data

The Data Intake tier also contains the required processing that can "PULL" data from external sources and also consume the "PUSHED" data from external sources.

The data sources from which data can be "PULLED" by the Intake tier include the following:

- Operational Data Stores ODS
- Data Warehouses
- Online Transaction Processing Systems (OLTP)
- NoSQL systems
- Mainframes
- Audio
- Video

Data sources that can "PUSH" data to the Intake tier include the following:

- Clickstream and machine logs such as Apache common logs
- Social media data from Twitter and so on
- Sensor data such as temperature, body sensors (Fitbit), and so on

The Transient Zone

A Transient landing zone is a predefined, secured intermediate location where the data from various source systems will be stored before moving it into the raw zone. Generally, the transient landing zone is a file-based storage where the data is organized by source systems. Record counts and file-size checks are carried out on the data in this zone before it is moved into the raw zone.

In the absence of a Transient Zone, the data will have to go directly from the external sources to the Raw Zone, which could severely hamper the quality of data in the Raw Zone. It also offers a platform for carrying out minimal data validation checks. Let us explore the following capabilities of the Transient Zone:

- A Transient Zone consolidates data from multiple sources, waits until a batch of data has "really" arrived, creates a basic aggregate by grouping together all the data from a single source, tags data with a metadata to indicate the source of origin, and generates timestamps and other relevant information.
- It performs a basic validity check on the data that has just arrived and signals the retry mechanism to kick in if the integrity of data is at question. MD5 checks and record counts can be employed to facilitate this step.

- It can even perform a high-level cleansing of data by removing/updating invalid data acquired from source systems (purely an optional step). It is a prime location for validating data quality from an external source for eventually auditing and tracking down data issues.

- It can support data archiving. There are situations in which the freshly acquired data is deemed not-so-important and thus can be relegated to an archive directly from the Transient Zone.

The following figure depicts the high-level functionality of the Transient Zone:

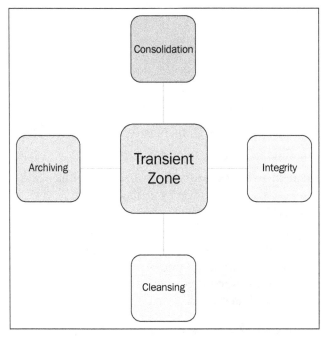

Transient Zone capabilities

The Raw Zone

The Raw Zone is a place where data lands from the Transient Zone. This is typically implemented as a file-based storage (Hadoop–HDFS). It includes a "Raw Data Storage" area to retain source data for the active use and archival. This is the zone where we have to consider storage options based on the timeliness of the data.

Batch Raw Storage

Batch intake data is commonly pull-based; we can leverage the power of HDFS to store massive amounts of data at a lower cost. The primary reason for the lower cost is that the data is stored on a low-cost commodity disk. One of the key advantages of Hadoop is its inherent ability to store data without the need for it to comply with any structure at the time of ingestion; the data can be refined and structured as and when needed. This schema-on-read ability avoids the need for upfront data modeling and costly **extract transform load** (**ETL**) processing of data before it is stored into the Raw Zone. Parallel processing is leveraged to rapidly place this data into the Raw Zone. The following are the key functionalities of this zone:

- This is the zone where data is deeply validated and watermarked to track and lineage lookup purposes.

- Metadata about the source data is also captured at this stage. Any relevant security attributes that have a say in the access control of the data are also captured as metadata. This process will ensure that history is rapidly accessible, enabling the tracking of metadata to allow users to easily understand where the data was acquired from and what types of enrichments are applied as information moves through the Data Lake.

- The Data Usage rights related to data governance are also captured and applied in this zone.

This zone enables reduced integration timeframes. In the traditional data warehouse model, information is consumed after it has been enriched, aggregated, and formatted to meet specific application needs. You can only consume the canned and aggregated data exhaust of a Data Warehouse. The Data Lake is architected differently to be modular, consisting of several distinct zones. These zones provide multiple consumption opportunities resulting in flexibility for the consumer. Applications needing minimal enrichment can access data from a zone (such as the Raw Zone) found early in the process workflow; bypassing "downstream" zones (such as the Data Hub Zone) reduces the cycle time to delivery. This is time-saving and can be significant to customers and consumers, such as data scientists with the need for fast-paced delivery and minimal enrichment.

The real-time Raw Storage

In many applications, it is mandatory to consume data and react to stimulus in real time. For these applications, the latency of writing the data to disk in a file-based system such as HDFS introduces unacceptable delay. Examples of these classes of applications as discussed earlier, include the GPS-aware mobile applications, or applications that have to respond to events from sensors. An in-memory solution called Gemfire can be used for real-time storage and to respond to events; it responds with a low latency and stores the data at rest in HDFS.

The following figure illustrates the choices we make in the Raw Zone based on the type of data:

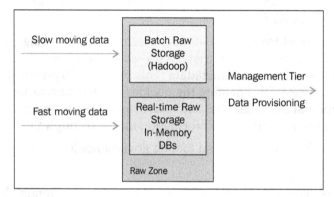

Raw Zone capabilities

The Data Management tier

In the preceding section, we discussed the ability of the Data Lake to intake and persist raw data as a precursor to prepare that data for migration to other zones of the Lake. In this section, we will see how that data moves from Raw to the Data Management tier in preparation for consumption and more sophisticated analytics.

The **Management tier** has three zones: the data flows sequentially from the Raw Zone to the Integration Zone through the Enrichment Zone and then finally after all the processes are complete, the final data is stored in a ready-to-use format in the Data Hub that is a combination of relational or NOSQL databases. The zones in the Management tier are as follows:

- The Integration Zone
- The Enrichment Zone
- The Data Hub Zone

As the data moves into the Management Zone, metadata is added and attached to each file. Metadata is a kind of watermark that tracks all changes made to each individual record. This tracking information, as well as activity logging and quality monitoring are stored in metadata that is persisted as the data moves through each of the zones. This information is extremely important to be able to report on the progress of the data through the Lake and will be used to expedite the investigation of anomalies and corrections needed to ensure quality information is delivered to the consuming applications. This metadata also helps in data discovery.

The Integration Zone

The Integration Zone's main functionality is to integrate various data and apply common transformations on the raw data into a standardized, cleansed structure that is optimized for data consumers. This zone eventually paves the way for storing the data into the Data Hub Zone. The key functionalities of the Integration Zone are as follows:

- Processes for automated data validation
- Processes for data quality checks
- Processes for integrity checks
- Associated operational management's audit logging and reporting

Here is a visual representation of the key functionalities of the Integration Zone:

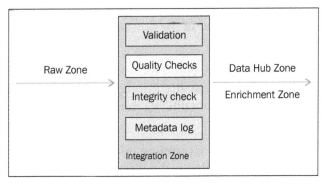

Integration Zone capabilities

The Enrichment Zone

The Enrichment Zone provides processes for data enhancement, augmentation, classification, and standardization. It includes processes for automated business rules' processing and processes to derive or append new attributes to the existing records from internal and external sources.

Integration and enrichments are performed on a file-based HDFS rather than a traditional relational data structure, because a file-based computing is advantageous — as the usage patterns of the data have not been determined yet, we have extreme flexibility within a file system. HDFS natively implements a schemaless storage system. The absence of a schema and indexes means you do not need to preprocess the data before you can use it. This means it loads faster and the structure is extensible, allowing it to flex as business needs change.

The following figure depicts the key functionalities of the Enrichment Zone:

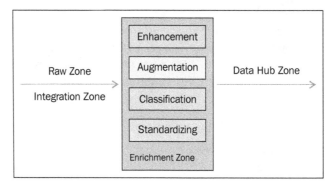

The Enrichment Zone's capabilities

The Data Hub Zone

The Data Hub Zone is the final storage location for cleaned and processed data. After the data is transformed and enriched in the downstream zones, it is finally pushed into the Data Hub for consumption.

The Data Hub is governed by a discovery process that is internally implemented as search, locate, and retrieve functionality through tools such as Elasticsearch or Solr/Lucene. A discovery is made possible by the extensive metadata that has been collected in the previous zones.

The data hub stores relational data in common relational databases such as Oracle and MS SQL server. It stores non-relational data in related technologies (for example, Hbase, Cassandra, MongoDB, Neo4J, and so on.)

The following figure depicts the capabilities of the Data Hub Zone:

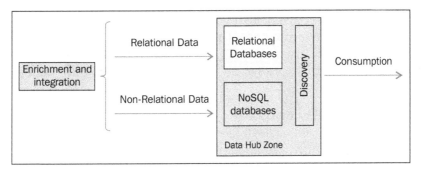

Data Hub Zone capabilities

The Data Consumption tier

In the preceding section, we discussed the capability of the zones in the Data Lake to move data from Raw to the Data Integration Zone. In this section, we will discuss the ways in which data is packaged and provisioned for consumption for more sophisticated analytics.

The **Consumption tier** is where the data is accessed either in raw format from the Raw Zone or in the structured format from the Data Hub. The data is provisioned through this tier for external access for analytics, visualization, or other application access through web services. The data is discovered by the data catalog published in the consumption zone and this actual data access is governed by security controls to limit unwarranted access.

The Data Discovery Zone

The Data Discovery Zone is the primary gateway for external users into the Data Lake. The key to implement a functional consumption tier is the amount and quality of Metadata that we would have collected in the preceding zones and the intelligent way in which we will expose this metadata for search and data retrieval. Too much governance on the metadata might miss the relevant search results and too little governance could jeopardize the security and integrity of the data.

Data discovery also uses data event logs that is a part of the Metadata, in order to query the data. All services that act on data in all the zones are logged along with their statuses, so that the consumers of data can understand the complete lineage of how data was impacted overtime. The Data Event Logging combined with metadata will enable extensive data discovery and allow users to explore and analyze data. In summary, this zone provides a facility to data consumers to browse, search, and discover the data.

Data discovery provides an interface to search data using the metadata or the data content. This interface provides flexible, self-driven data discovery capabilities that enable the users to efficiently find and analyze relevant information.

The Data Provisioning Zone

Data Provisioning allows data consumers to source/consume the data that is available in the Data Lake. This tier is designed to allow you to use the metadata that specify the "publications" that need to be created, the "subscription" specific customization requirements, and the end delivery of the requested data to the "data consumer." The Data Provisioning is done on the entire data that is residing in the Data Lake. The data that is provisioned can be either in the Raw Zone or in the Data Hub Zone.

The following figure depicts the important features of the Consumption tier:

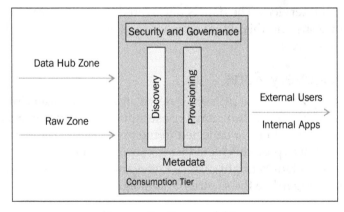

Consumption Zone capabilities

Summary

This chapter has emphasized the need for Data Lake implementation in an enterprise context and has provided a practical guidance on when to go for a Data Lake. We can now comprehend the significant benefits a Data Lake offers over a traditional Data warehouse kind of implementation.

In the later sections, we introduced you to the Data Lake concept and its essentials. We then covered the various layers of a Data Lake and provided an overview of its architectural components and details of how crucial each of these components are in building a successful Data Lake.

In the next chapter, you will understand the Data Intake component and the functionalities that can be enabled for this component. It provides architectural guidance and delves deeper into the various Big Data tools and technologies that can be used for building this component.

2
Data Intake

In the preceding chapter, you understood the need for Data Lake and gained a high-level understanding of the key components that can comprise a Data Lake and how important each of these components are for building it. We have seen how the changing business landscape is provoking data growth and how organizations are adopting a newer paradigm such as Data Lake to ingest this data and extract analytical value.

In this chapter, you will understand in detail, the Intake Tier that was introduced in *Chapter 1, The Need for Data Lake*. The following topics will be covered in this chapter:

- The process of obtaining data into the Data Lake's Intake Tier
- An high level overview of the various External Data Sources from which the data can be acquired, and the variety of data that can be ingested
- The key functionalities that can be implemented as part of the Data Intake Tier
- The various data intake modes
- Big Data tools and technologies that can be used to acquire a variety of data from external sources; architectural guidance on choosing the tools for Data Intake

The following figure represents the end state architecture of the Data Lake as discussed in *Chapter 1, The Need for Data Lake*. In the subsequent sections, we will be discussing in detail, the highlighted Intake Tier of the Data Lake end-state architecture:

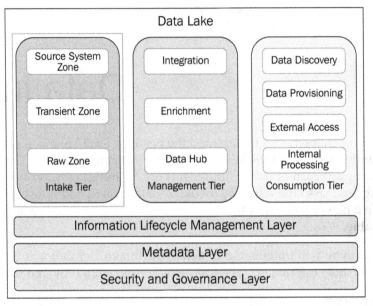

Data Lake end-state architecture

Understanding Intake tier zones

Enterprises sit on vast reserves of diverse, potentially invaluable data such as databases, social media, logs, and sensor data locked in data silos. The Data Lake is schema-less and stores data of any type and format. Not only storing, but offering the ability to integrate data from disparate sources and ingest high-velocity, multi-structured and massive datasets. This key feature empowers enterprises to perform exploratory and advanced data analysis on all the data and quickly gain actionable insights.

Before the Data Lake is utilized to its hilt to perform data analysis, there should be mechanisms implemented to seamlessly connect the Data Lake to various external data sources and acquire data from them. The Intake Tier in the Data Lake architecture implements the functionalities needed to address this. In the following subsection, let us study the Intake Tier in detail.

Let us start by understanding the data flow from the **External Data Sources** to the Intake Tier. The following figure illustrates the data flow to the Data Intake Tier:

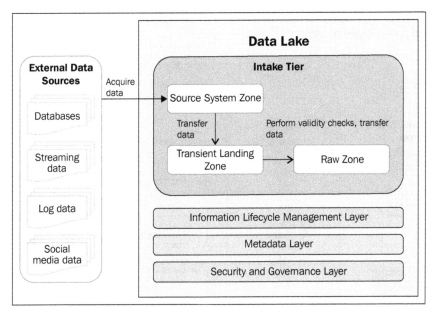

Flow of data in Data Intake Tier

In the preceding image, the data flows in the following order:

1. The **Source System Zone** establishes the connectivity to the **External Data Sources**.

2. It accesses the data, extracts the required data, and transfers the data into the **Transient Landing Zone** for it to perform basic validity checks.

3. After the validity checks have been performed, the data is moved into the **Raw Zone** to make it accessible for further processing.

The following sections help you understand the features of each zone in the Intake Tier.

Source System Zone functionalities

This section introduces the Source System Zone and helps you to understand its various features.

The Source System Zone abstracts the connectivity and processing services that are needed to acquire data from the External Data Sources. This zone provides the interfaces required to implement all the connections to external file shares, databases, and sensor devices. The data can be acquired using various time-based acquisition strategies such as real-time acquisition or batch acquisition, and the data can be loaded incrementally or all at once.

The following image gives you a quick snapshot of the functionalities that can be performed in the Source System Zone:

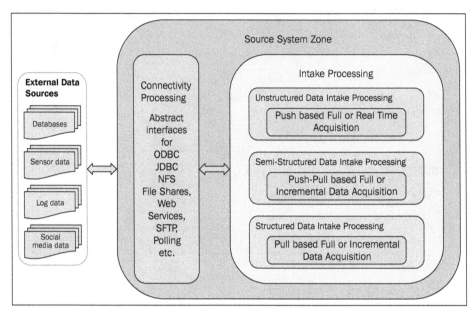

Source System Zone functionalities

Understanding connectivity processing

The connectivity layer in the Source System Zone implements mechanisms to connect to a variety of external data sources such as databases, social media chatter, logs, and sensor. Each of these data sources differ in the way they have to be accessed, connected, polled, and retried, and eventually their respective data is acquired.

Some of the key functionalities and interfaces implemented by this layer are as follows:

- Establishing connectivity to structured databases
- Establishing connectivity to file shares
- Periodically polling for the availability of data from external sources
- Establishing connectivity to web resources such as SFTP and REST APIs
- Establishing connectivity to sensors, devices, and cloud platforms
- Establishing connectivity to social media APIs such as Twitter
- Connection pooling, connection retry, and time-out mechanisms

Once the connectivity layer has established the connectivity with External Data Sources, the **Intake Processing** performs the actual data acquisition.

In the next section, we will understand how this is accomplished by understanding it within the context of data variety.

Understanding Intake Processing for data variety

This section takes you through an overview of the data variety, helps you understand why it is important to integrate a variety of data in the Data Lake, and also highlights the role of the Source System Zone in performing Intake Processing.

The Source System Zone's Intake Processing performs a key role in data acquisition, which includes the processing steps that are needed to do the following:

- Poll external data sources for the availability of data
- Acquire data into the Data Lake whenever it is pushed
- Acquire vast amounts of file-based data in batch mode
- Acquire data incrementally (through change data capture)
- Queue real-time streaming data
- Attempt retries or notify whenever data is not acquired properly
- Scale horizontally whenever the acquired data sizes shoot beyond a limit
- Load balance; recover from disasters so that the data is not lost
- Acknowledge or verify the data transfer through handshake mechanisms

The following subsections help you comprehend the details of how the Source System Zone aids in intake processing of various types of data.

Structured data

Structured data is neatly arranged by delimiters so that a machine can understand its structure; it has entities that have a well-defined format and follow a predefined schema. The data is defined by a set of attributes or fields with their data type specifying the type of data each attribute can hold. A few examples of structured data are as follows:

- Data from Online Transaction Processing systems
- Point-of-sale data
- Mainframe data
- Enterprise Resource Planning data
- Data in the form of flat delimited files

The need for integrating Structured Data in the Data Lake

Ingesting structured data from varied sources into the Data Lake enables the integration of data from proliferating databases, transactional systems such as ERP and CRM systems, and legacy systems such as mainframes. This integration eliminates data silos; all of the data on the Data Lake can now be utilized to get a coherent view that can power a new generation of data-aware applications.

Structured data loading approaches

The Source System Zone typically *Pulls* structured data from the External Data Sources by connecting to the data sources, polling it at regular intervals to check for available data, and then initiating the process of actually acquiring the data. All these functionalities are abstracted in the Source System Zone and are implemented specific to the External Data Source.

The process of acquiring the data can be either a full data load or an incremental one as follows:

- **Full Data Load**: The Source System Zone performs full data load when the data is acquired for the first time. The data from the External Data Source is acquired completely so that the data in the Data Intake Tier reflects the snapshot of the data that is available in the External Data Source.

- **Incremental Data Load**: Incremental data load is performed by the Source System Zone to load the changes in the external data source that have occurred since the last successful data import. Here are a few strategies to implement Incremental Data Load:

  - **Time stamps**: Time stamps stored in the database tables can be used to identify new or modified data.

  - **Partitioning**: Range partitioning can be performed on the source table to partition it along a partitioning key such as date; this allows easy identification of the new data.

  - **Change tables**: Change Data Capture (CDC) can be enabled in databases to populate change tables that maintain a record of all the changes. These changes can be extracted from the source system.

  - **Triggers**: Triggers can be used to watch the recently updated records and to update the last modified time stamp value with the current time. Thus, the time stamp column always holds the latest time and date when a given record was last modified.

Semi-structured data

Semi-structured data is just like structured data, but it does not respect the structural constraints at all times. Most of the time semi-structured data is loosely coupled to the enforced schema, and uses the schema as a guide to the structure of the data. The schema in the semi-structured data varies from record to record. Typically, semi-structured data is used to represent complex relationships using a nested approach; this nesting cannot usually be intuitively depicted using relational databases. A few examples of semi-structured data are as follows:

- Data stored or exchanged in JSON, RDF, or XML format
- Application-generated log data
- Clickstream data

The need for integrating semi-structured data in the Data Lake

The ingestion of semi-structured data such as application and web logs into the Data Lake and integrating them with machine data or network logs can help identify hidden patterns from it. These hidden patterns can be analyzed to predict machine failures and gain Operational Intelligence (OI).

Semi-structured data loading approaches

The Source System Zone acquires semi-structured data either by *Pulling* data from the External Data Sources or waiting until the data is *Pushed* into this zone.

In both cases of Pull and Push, the Source System Zone connects to the External Data Sources and initiates the process of actually acquiring the data. The major difference between Pull and Push is that; with Push, the External Data Sources *Push* the data to the Source System Zone whenever the data is available. Whereas, while *Pulling* the data, the Source System Zone periodically polls the External Data Source for data availability before acquiring the data.

In either cases of Pull or Push, the process of acquiring the data can be either a full data load or an incremental one, as described in the preceding subsection.

Unstructured data

Unstructured data does not conform to any particular predefined internal structure or data model. It is organized in a haphazard way that makes it difficult to parse by traditional approaches. A few examples are as follows:

- Unstructured data in a textual form such as documents, e-mails, and social chatter
- Machine-generated data such as RFID data, sensor data, and so on
- Binary data sources such as medical images, Youtube videos, or audio files

The need for integrating Unstructured data in the Data Lake

The unstructured data that is ingested from many sources, such as social media chatter and clickstreams, can be integrated with historical data on the Data Lake and provisioned to downstream analytical systems. By applying real-time analytics to this data, organizations can gain significant insights that aid in real-time decision making.

Unstructured data loading approaches

The Source System Zone typically loads unstructured data in continuous streams or a batch depending on the type of data.

Data such as machine logs, sensors, and so on, are *Pushed* into the Source System Zone whenever they are generated.

Unstructured data such as documents, images, and videos, are generally loaded into the Data Intake Tier all at once, just like the full load. These specific data types are generally *Pulled* or *Pushed* into the Source System Zone.

The Source System Zone has connection-processing mechanisms that connect to external data sources, that listen/wait for these logs/events/files, queues them, and finally acquires the data.

Transient Landing Zone functionalities

This section introduces and helps you understand various processing steps such as validations and integrity checks that are performed on the data while it is residing in the Transient Landing Zone.

The Transient Landing Zone is a predefined, secure intermediate location where the data acquired from various External Data Sources will be stored before moving it into the Raw Zone. In the case of batch processing, all the events or data arriving at a periodic interval can be stored into a file. For real-time processing scenarios, the events are streamed into the system, validated in the Transient Landing Zone, and consumed by the subsequent tiers to execute processing on it. Generally, the Transient Landing Zone is a file system-based storage where the data is organized by External Data Sources. Record counts and file-size checks are carried out on the data in this zone before it is moved into the Raw Zone.

The following image gives you a quick snapshot of the steps that could be performed in the Transient Landing Zone:

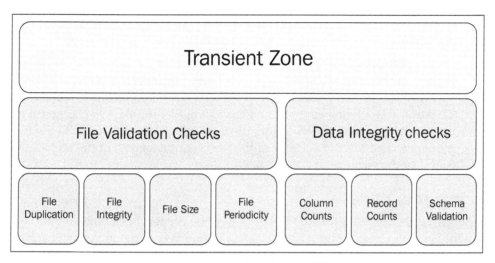

Transient Landing Zone functionalities

File validation checks

File validation checks are performed to ensure that duplicate files are not ingested, file integrity is maintained, and to check that files are being received at periodic intervals. In this subsection, let us go through each of the processing steps that comprise file validation checks.

File duplication checks

File duplication checks are carried out at the Transient Landing Zone in the Intake Tier to ensure that duplicate files are not ingested into the Data Lake. File duplication occurs in cases where incremental data is loaded at periodic intervals; the same data is received in the Transient Landing Zone that was ingested in the previous intake cycle from the same external source.

The deduplication process checks the incoming files for duplicates; it is a three step process listed as follows:

1. **Compare file names**: The file name of the incoming file is compared against the file name of the file that already exists in the Data Lake; if the name is the same, then it is flagged as a duplicate suspect and the next check is performed on it.

2. **Compare the schema**: The schema of the duplicate suspect incoming file is validated with the schema of the file with the same file name that is already stored in the Data Lake. If the schema is the same, then the file is still a duplicate suspect and the next step of checking the content is performed. If the schemas do not match, the file is no more a duplicate suspect.

3. **Compare the content**: This step finds out whether the incoming duplicate suspect file is really a duplicate by comparing the checksum of the incoming file with the file that is already stored in the Data Lake and that has the same file name and schema as that of the incoming file. If the MD5 checksum of the files match, then the incoming file is flagged as a duplicate and the file is deleted. The MD5 checksum of the file is stored as part of the metadata to enable deduplication.

File integrity checks

File integrity checks are performed to verify that the file has been received at the Transient Landing Zone without any errors in transmission; the integrity is verified by using message digests. The message digest of the file that is being transferred can be calculated at the External Data Source and sent as part of the metadata when the file is pushed for ingestion. After the data intake is complete, the message digest of the received file is calculated in the Transient Landing Zone and is compared with the value sent by the External Data Source. If the values do not match, the file integrity is lost and the appropriate actions, such as reinitiation of the intake or sending notifications for manual intervention can be performed.

File size checks

The file size of the file that is being transferred can be calculated at the external data source; this file size would be part of the metadata when the file is pushed for ingestion. The file size on the external source can be validated at the Transient Landing Zone after the data intake is complete at the Data Lake. If the file size does not match, the files have to be flagged appropriately and the next course of action, such as reinitiation of the intake or sending notifications for a manual intervention can be performed.

File periodicity checks

File periodicity checks ensure files are received at periodic intervals: Automated checks can be put in place to monitor directories where the files would be ingested at periodic intervals. If the files are not being ingested, this process would send alerts or notifications informing that files are not being ingested.

Data Integrity checks

Data Integrity checks are carried out on the data at the time of data intake in order to ensure that all the data that was ingested from an External Data Source has been received at the Transient Landing Zone successfully without losing its integrity. The following sections discuss a few techniques used for Data Integrity checking.

Checking record counts

Validating record counts ensures Data Integrity and enables identification of missing records, if any. While acquiring data from External Data Sources such as databases, the record counts can be calculated at the external source and captured as part of the metadata. In the case of structured delimited files, the record counts on the external data source will be part of the metadata while the file is ingested. These record counts are matched at the Transient Landing Zone after the Data Intake is complete. If the record counts do not match, the respective files are flagged appropriately and the next course of action such as reinitiation of the intake or sending notifications for a manual intervention can be performed.

Checking for column counts

The number of columns that are part of data extraction can be captured and stored as part of the metadata. The column count on the external source is validated with the column count on the Transient Landing Zone after the intake process is complete. If the column counts do not match, the files are flagged appropriately and the next course of action such as reinitiation of the intake or sending notifications for a manual intervention can be performed.

Schema validation checks

Schema validation checks are performed on the data in the Transient Landing Zone to validate if there are any structural changes in the schema of the External Data Source since the last data ingestion.

The structure of the data in the Transient Landing Zone is changed whenever there are any structural changes detected in the External Data Source. This ensures that the new data that gets ingested has the same structure as it is in the external source. Avro or Thrift can be used for schema evolution.

Raw Storage Zone functionalities

This section introduces and helps you understand various functionalities of the Raw Storage Zone. These functionalities help capture deep metadata, prevent degradation of data when it is stored for a longer duration, by performing deep bit-level integrity checks and periodic checksums, and enable security and governance mechanisms on the data while it is residing in the Raw Storage Zone.

The Raw Storage Zone is a part of the Data Intake Tier. After validating the incoming records for duplication, schema changes, and integrity in the Transient Landing Zone, the data is ingested into the Raw Storage Zone. This zone contains raw data in its original form, with the original fidelity of the data being preserved. This data is retained for active use and archiving, and will be made available for discovery and provisioning, making it accessible to any downstream systems that require the raw data for performing analytical processing. Deep validation of data is performed here and this data is watermarked for lineage and tracking.

The following image gives you a quick snapshot of the steps that could be performed in the Raw Storage Zone:

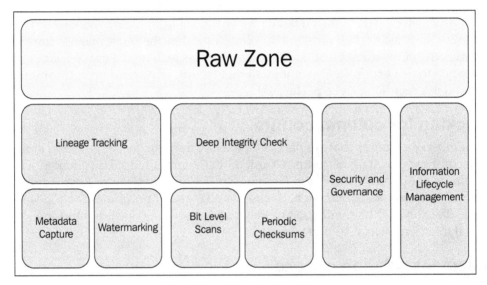

Raw Storage Zone functionalities

Data lineage processes

The following subsections help you in understanding the processes that are performed on the data in the Raw Zone to capture data lineage and enable **Lineage Tracking**.

Watermarking process

Watermarking is a specific process performed on structured data to track its lineage. It is applied on the data in the Raw Zone where a unique identifier is appended to each record. It enables to capture changes that were made to the record using this unique identifier. This helps in tracking the complete lifecycle of the data as it moves overtime through various tiers/zones in the Data Lake.

Metadata capture

In this context, Metadata is captured for structured, semi-structured, and unstructured data in the Raw Storage Zone. It collects vital information about the history and provenance of data by capturing information on when the data was ingested into the Data Lake, who initiated the ingestion, and where the data originated from.

The following list gives you a brief overview of the range of information that could be captured as metadata:

- The external data source information.

- The entity information such as table names with row counts, column data type information in case of relational sources or file names, the MD5 checksum of the file, the date and time of ingestion, the destination details, and the retention period.

- A data dictionary can be built at this stage where the metadata is captured from the business perspective. Each attribute in business terms is defined and this enables easy exploration of data during data discovery.

This metadata is a means of cataloguing the existing data on the Data Lake to enable data discovery and track the lineage of data to know how data moves from the initial raw form across the data pipeline. Metadata capture will be discussed in detail in *Chapter 5, Data Governance*.

Deep Integrity checks

As we have seen in *Chapter 1, The Need for Data Lake*, the data in the Raw Zone is deeply validated. The following integrity checks can be performed on the data.

Bit Level Integrity checks

Data corruption might happen on the physical storage media such as the hard disks of the Hadoop cluster nodes. When the data is stored for an extended period of time, it tends to get corrupted; this is known as bit rot.

Blocks that comprise a file can be verified periodically to detect any corruption. The checksum of the block is compared with the original checksum and bad blocks can be identified. These bad blocks are identified and replaced as and when they are detected so that the file level integrity is maintained at all times.

Periodic checksum checks

A checksum can be used to detect the loss of data integrity. The checksum of the data in the Raw Storage Zone is calculated and stored as part of the metadata. The checksum is verified on all subsequent reads to ensure that data integrity is maintained.

The checksum of the data can be periodically validated against the original checksum to detect data corruption.

There are multiple integrity assurance techniques, **Mirroring** is one such technique where two or more copies of data are maintained. If the loss of data integrity is detected, the corrupted data can be replaced with the copy of good data.

Security and governance

Data security and access groups requiring access to the data, which is at rest and in-flight by users, applications, and the network, can be identified and the appropriate policies can be defined on who can access what data. Sensitive data can be identified and masked in this zone to comply with the enterprise policies. Governance would be applied on the data by having the security policies in place to enable authenticated and authorized access to the data in both the Transient and Raw Zones. This is performed as a part of the Security and Governance layer and will be discussed in detail in *Chapter 5, Data Governance*.

Information Lifecycle Management

Retention period is normally defined in the Raw Storage Zone; it states the use-by-date of the data. This is performed as a part of the Information Lifecycle Management layer. Generally, when data is stored for longer periods, its value decreases and the storage cost increases overtime. Defining retention periods and policies enables the Information lifecycle management layer to leverage tools that can archive, down-tier, or purge the data.

Practical Data Ingestion scenarios

Now that we have understood the Data Intake tier in detail, let us get a feel of how it is implemented in real-life situations when specifically dealing with Big Data. Here is a compilation of a few cases:

- A product-based company has huge structured data assets; their goal is to leverage data from external sources to improve their user experience. To address this, they have built a Big Data solution that ingests data from their structured data sources and social networks that have data about the preferences, needs, and opinions of their users. The data from social media is integrated and analyzed with the enterprise's structured data to understand user preferences and glean insights on their products based on the user's opinion. This helped them to improve their user experience and increased sales.

- A leading credit card issuing bank has implemented a Big Data solution that ingests huge volumes of batch data such as past activity, credit history, geographical information, spending habits, trends, and real-time data such as transactional data into the Data Lake. All of this data is analyzed using a fraud detection algorithm that analyses each transaction in real time, matches it with historical data, checks for patterns and sends out alerts if the algorithm identifies patterns that indicate any suspicious or fraudulent activity.

Architectural guidance

This section attempts to answer one key question: which tool should be used for which use case and how do we decide the best option?

As evidenced in the previous sections, there are a plethora of options available for establishing connectivity to External Data Sources and Ingesting data into the Data Lake's Intake Tier.

Choosing a tool for ingestion depends primarily on the use case you are attempting to implement using the Data Lake. Many implementations of Data Lake end up using multiple tools together to acquire and process data. We also see that the market is flooded with umpteen numbers of tools that make decision making very difficult.

In this section, we will try to provide a crisp overview of the things to be considered while selecting a tool. This is by no means an exhaustive coverage, but it tries to give you enough depth so that you will be in a decent position to extrapolate using this knowledge and make better decisions.

The choice of the tool invariably starts with the now ever-obvious use cases, which can be broadly categorized into two major groups based on the type of data to be ingested.

Structured data use cases

All the Data Lake use cases that derive insights by integrating with operational systems or enterprise data warehouses, to perform traditional business intelligence, feed OLAP applications and generate basic visualization such as reports and drilldowns that ingest Structured Data into the Data Lake's Intake Tier. The ingestion of structured data can be scheduled to be performed at regular intervals. Most of this data is *Pulled* from External Data Sources. The tools available to ingest data for this category of use cases are Sqoop and WebHDFS, for ingesting delimited files, Splunk (to an extent), and so on.

Semi-structured and unstructured data use cases

These are advanced use cases of implementing a Data Lake to wring the last drop of value from the data assets within and without the organization. For instance, if the businesses' use case need analytic insights from the following:

- Performing social media analysis
- Building recommendation engines for e-commerce sites
- Advanced visualization techniques such as Heat Map and Tag Cloud
- Analyzing In-memory event streams
- Acquiring sensor data and detecting anomalies in real time
- Conducting simulations on massive behavioral data

In all of the preceding business use cases, you were dealing with mostly unstructured data that has to be ingested into the Data Lake as soon as possible to generate insights. These use cases typically ingest on the fly data such as sensor exhaust, social chatter, clickstreams, and so on.

There are a few other use cases such as natural language processing of voluminous text, for which the speed of ingest for unstructured data doesn't really matter.

The tools available to ingest data for these categories of use cases are Flume, Kafka Storm, Fluentd, and Splunk, and so on.

The following figure simplifies this decision-making process by taking into consideration the preceding combinations and suggests an indicative list of tools that can be used for each use case:

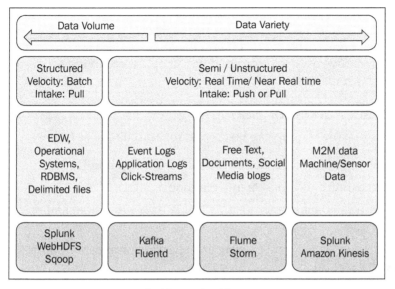

Architectural guidance

This list of Big Data tools and technologies can then be evaluated to see whether they fit in for the specific use case requirement in your organization's context. The next section details out each of the tools.

Big Data tools and technologies

Now that we have understood the various aspects of the Data Intake tier, the following sections provide an overview of Big Data tools for ingesting structured, semi-structured, and unstructured data as discussed in the preceding section.

Ingestion of structured data

Let us now explore a few Big Data technologies used for ingesting structured data from relational databases and structured delimited files into the Data Lake.

Sqoop

Sqoop, a Hadoop ecosystem component, allows you to efficiently transfer peta-byte scale data between RDBMS and Hadoop. This tool helps to acquire the data from RDBMS, by efficiently interacting with traditional RDBMS servers to perform the import and export of data. Loading peta-byte scale data into the Data Lake from production databases is a challenging task as it involves the overhead of handling issues such as data consistency, failure handling, and parallelism, and this is where Sqoop excels.

With Sqoop, you can perform full data extraction, bulk data extraction, CDC, and online or offline extraction. Sqoop allows you to select particular columns or filter particular rows from a table to load it into the Data Intake Tier. It also supports CDC, that is able to retrieve only the rows that were not present in the set of rows that were previously imported.

Use case scenarios for Sqoop

The scenarios in which Sqoop can be used to ingest data are as follows:

- Ingest structured data from relational databases into Hadoop

- Ingest mainframe datasets into Hadoop

- Perform full data extraction, CDC, bulk data extraction, and online or offline extraction

- Extract a subset of data by selecting specific columns or filter rows to match a condition

 A compact data format such as Avro can be used in combination with compression when you are importing massive amounts of data. Compression codecs can be passed as arguments to compress the files according to the codec of your choice.

 More information on Sqoop can be found at the following URL: http://sqoop.apache.org/docs/1.4.6/index.html

WebHDFS

In Data Lake, there are external upstream systems that use a *Push*-based approach to ingest data into HDFS. To ingest the data without the need for Hadoop to be installed on these systems, they will need access to the HDFS and the data stored in it; WebHDFS was developed to address this need.

WebHDFS allows external clients to access Hadoop in a language-agnostic way; it retains native Hadoop protocol security and inherent parallelism that Hadoop offers. All the HDFS operations are supported by WebHDFS.

Use case scenarios for WebHDFS

WebHDFS can be used in use cases where there is a need to do the following:

- Ingestion of structured as well as unstructured files into HDFS in a batch or streaming mode, without the need for Hadoop to be installed on the client
- Steady addition of data into log files.

 More information on WebHDFS can be found at the following URL: `https://hadoop.apache.org/docs/r1.0.4/webhdfs.html`

Ingestion of streaming data

The following subsections provide an overview of a few Big Data technologies used for ingesting large-scale streaming data.

Apache Flume

Apache Flume addresses the need for collecting, aggregating, and ingesting large-scale streaming data into the Data Lake's Intake Tier. Flume was designed to be distributed; it is robust, fault-tolerant, and reliable.

Flume collects streaming data in a centralized store, primarily Hadoop. This streaming data can be utilized to perform real-time analysis or batch analysis depending upon the use case.

Use case scenarios for Flume

Flume can be used in use cases where there is a need to ingest real-time or micro batch data such as application logs, network protocols, IoT devices, and social media data into the Data Lake's Intake Tier

 More information on Flume can be found at the following URL: `https://flume.apache.org/releases/1.6.0.html`

Fluentd

Fluentd was developed to address the collection and transport aspects of centralized logging; it provides a unified logging layer that abstracts data sources from backend systems.

Fluentd supports file and memory-based buffering to prevent data loss. It has a plugin system that allows easy extensibility to read from multiple sources and write to multiple sinks.

Use case scenarios for Fluentd

Fluentd can be used in use cases where there is a need to ingest real-time or micro batch data such as application logs, network protocols, IoT devices, and social media data into the Data Lake's Intake Tier.

More information on Fluentd can be found at the following URL: http://docs.fluentd.org/articles/quickstart

Kafka

Kafka was built as a unified platform to address the need to handle real-time data feeds and integrate these feeds with external data sources. Kafka provides scalable, fast, and persistent messaging that enables parallel data loads into the Data Lake.

Huge amounts of terabyte scale data can be ingested by Kafka, allowing the implementation of use cases that cannot be handled by traditional systems.

Use case scenarios for Kafka

Kafka can be used in use cases where there is a need to ingest real-time or micro batch data such as application logs, network protocols, IoT devices, and social media data into the Data Lake's Intake Tier.

More information on Kafka can be found at the following URL: http://kafka.apache.org/documentation.html

Amazon Kinesis

Kinesis provides the ability to aggregate and store terabytes of data from multiple sources such as clickstreams, social media data, logs, GPS tracking, and financial transactions data to perform real-time processing on it. Kinesis supports the consumption of the data by multiple applications that can perform various actions simultaneously and independently.

Use case scenarios for Kinesis

Kinesis can be used in use cases where there is a need to set up high-capacity data pipes to rapidly ingest real-time data such as clickstreams, social media data, logs, GPS tracking, and financial transactions data into the Data Lake's Intake Tier.

 More information on Kinesis can be found at the following URL:
`http://aws.amazon.com/kinesis/developer-resources/`

Apache Storm

Storm is an event processing system built to rapidly ingest data from event streams and is often used to acquire data into Data Lake's Hadoop storage and OLAP systems.

Storm is data type agnostic and processes any data type; any programming language can use Storm. It guarantees that stream processing happens without data loss.

Use case scenarios for Storm

Storm can be used in use cases where there is a need to rapidly ingest real-time data such as clickstreams, social media data, logs, GPS tracking, and financial transactions data into the Data Lake's Intake Tier.

 More information on Storm can be found at the following URL:
`https://storm.apache.org/documentation/Home.html`

Summary

This chapter explained the Data Intake layer in detail; we started with understanding the various zones in the Intake tier and the external sources from which the data can be acquired as per your use case. We then took a deep dive into the functionalities of the Source System Zone, Transient landing Zone, and the Raw Zone and also comprehended the best practices that can be considered while architecting the Data Intake tier.

In the subsequent sections, we took a look at the various Big Data tools and technologies that can be used to acquire different types of data from various sources. The architectural guidance section helped you in decision making in order to arrive at the set of technologies that can be used for specific use cases.

In the next chapter, you will understand the Data Integration, Quality, and Enrichment zones; it will take you through the key functionalities of these zones and provides architectural guidance on how to go about implementing these zones.

3
Data Integration, Quality, and Enrichment

In the preceding chapter, we understood the details of obtaining huge volumes of data into the Data Lake's Intake Tier from various External Data Sources. We learned various Hadoop-oriented data transfer mechanisms to either; pull the data from sources or push the data in near real-time, and to perform historical or incremental loads. We also saw the key functionalities that are implemented as part of the Data Intake Tier and got architectural guidance on the Big Data tools and technologies.

Now that the data has been acquired into the Data Lake, we will explore the next logical steps that are performed on the data in this chapter. In a nutshell, we will take a closer look at the Management Tier and understand how to efficiently manage the vast amounts of data and deliver it to multiple applications and systems with a high degree of performance and scalability.

In this chapter, we will gain a deeper understanding of the following topics:

- The key components in the Management Tier: Data Transformation, Data Enrichment, and storage in the Data Hub.
- Learn how to perform Data Enrichment and Data Transformations and also the use of Hadoop ecosystem components.

Introduction to the Data Management Tier

The key purpose of the Management Tier is to acquire data from the Raw Zone of the Intake Tier and package it so that the data is ready for exploration, discovery, provisioning, and consumption by the end users or applications. The Management tier is a logical intermediary that bridges the gap between the raw data available in the Intake Tier and the discovery efforts performed in the Consumption Tier.

It is important to recollect that most of the steps in the Management Tier are potentially optional. In many practical implementations of the Data Lake, it is evidenced that the data is directly consumed from the Raw Zone of the Intake Tier. This is true in cases where the raw data is needed for data exploration and building analytical models. Hence, in such cases, all the steps that are part of the Management Tier are deemed optional.

The following figure represents the end-state architecture of the Data Lake as discussed in *Chapter 1, The Need for Data Lake*. In the subsequent sections, we will discuss in detail the highlighted Management Tier of the Data Lake end-state architecture:

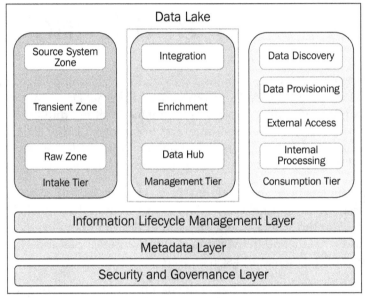

Data Lake end-state architecture

In the preceding figure, the Management Tier has three zones, in which the data flows from the Raw Zone of the Intake Tier to the **Integration** zone through the **Enrichment** zone and then finally the data is stored in a ready-to-use format in the **Data Hub**, which is actually a combination of relational or No-SQL databases.

Understanding Data Integration

In this section, let us dive deeper into and understand the underlying concepts of Data Integration.

Introduction to Data Integration

In the previous chapter, we saw that the data in the Intake Tier is in its native format with no operations performed on the data to check for its validity.

To make real use of this newly acquired data in its native format, it has to be combined or integrated with the historical data assets residing within the Enterprise Data Centre to improve the success of gathering analytical insights.

The practical goal of Data Integration is to provide a unified view through a single access point to all the data that is residing or that can be accessed by the Data Lake. Without this capability, there would be chaos, due to the multiple access points of the data; without this capability, organizations cannot integrate multiple sources, enrich it, and deliver it to data consumers rapidly to maximize its competitive advantage.

Data Lake's Integration capability is touted as the most efficient way to combine data from an array of large-volume and high-velocity data sources. The Integration of newly acquired data can be performed with data residing in internal data sources such as mainframes, Operational Data Sources, and Enterprise Data Warehouses along with data from External Data Sources.

Using the Data Lake's Integration capability, you may expect the following practical gains:

- Static data assets of the organization are combined with real-time market trends, using which Business Intelligence applications can perform enhanced query and report functionalities on business activities

- Enterprise-wide planning and optimization can be done on the population of data instead of performing it on a sample so that advanced statistical analysis techniques and data mining can be performed

- Customer relationship management can be enhanced by analyzing unstructured clickstream data such as customer behavior, along with structured business trends and current sales

- Viral marketing campaigns' penetration can be enhanced by integrating data about customers and their behavioral profiles derived from social media analysis

Integration of data includes steps that discover the native data, perform quality checks and cleanse it, perform transformations on it, enrich the data, monitor all these steps, and package the data for consumption.

The following figure depicts the Data Integration architecture:

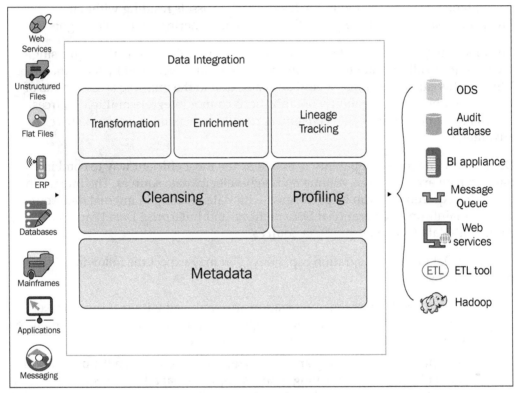

Data Integration architecture

Prominent features of Data Integration

In order to maximize the potential of extracting value from the data stored in the Data Lake, we would suggest that the following features are implemented.

Loosely coupled Integration

The Data Lake stores structured and unstructured data such as videos, e-mails, presentations, and web pages, which constitute 70-80 percent of all the data. The data Integration capability will do well if it is designed in a loosely coupled fashion that enables dynamic, just-in-time integration of the structured and unstructured data. This capability adapts well with changing business needs and minimizes upfront processing costs.

Ease of use

The Data Lake, being the repository of all the streams of data, can perform the best if it is designed in a flexible way for nonexperts to load data, integrate it with other sources, and extract insights. Sometimes, it is not only the data scientists and the data wranglers that benefit from insights, but also common users who are typically experts on the subject matter and can throw some light on the data with their insights. It is for these business-oriented folks, that we can design the Data Lake's Integration capability to manage and share their data and views with the ease to enable them to incrementally and collaboratively build an integrated dataset for analytics.

Secure access

As discussed in the preceding point, providing ease of access to data to literally anyone doesn't imply that we have to compromise on the security and integrity of the data. The Data Lake's Integration capability would be improved if it was implemented with a sense of security that is flexible and effective at the same time. Even though Data Integration provides numerous benefits in terms of better insights, accessing and sharing of data is hampered by privacy and security concerns. Data Lake's Integration capability can balance the flexibility in providing data access with robust techniques that guarantee privacy.

High-quality data

The integrated data that flows in from many sources into the Data Lake, makes real business sense if only it meets stringent data quality parameters. No matter how many sources we integrate from, the Data Lake is simply worthless if there is no way to transform substandard data and make it accurate, complete, and consistent in a timely fashion. The Data Lake's Integration capability will be improved if it encompasses ways to detect low-quality data and perform appropriate transformations on it. Workflows can be put in motion to assess the External Data Sources and consumers for their quality compliance. Some techniques such as ontology-embedded schemas and OWL-RDFs can be used to ensure that the quality is maintained across integration sources.

Lineage tracking

Many times, the end users of the data in the Data Lake need to know and verify where the data originated from, how it was integrated, and how it was transformed; this knowledge builds trust in the data and the resultant insights. Also, this knowledge enables traceability of a fault to the original source, which can be an External Data Source or a transformation process.

Practical Data Integration scenarios

Now that we have understood the important aspects of Data Integration, in this section, let us get a feel of what Data Integration does in real-life situations when specifically dealing with Big Data. Here is a compilation of various cases:

- In recent times, we have seen a spate of regulatory measures for the financial institutions across the world. For instance, the banks to be compliant to the Basel II standard; they have to precisely access the credit risks of all the customers. Currently, the data is scattered in silos in various departmental Data Warehouses and there is no way to get a comprehensive and integrated access to customer data. Added to this, customer behavior data is typically extracted from clickstreams and social conversations; using traditional approaches, there is no way to store, integrate, and analyze this data in conjunction with the structured customer data. The Data Lake's Integration capability can enable the banks to combine any and all the data for a comprehensive view of structured and unstructured data on customers and help build better predictive credit risk models that operate on the population rather than the sample. The following two cases illustrate the practical scenarios:

  - A US-based banking giant processes 40,000 TB complex transformations per second on its consumer records to understand customer behavioral patterns and better assess credit risks

  - A banking conglomerate based out of Europe runs transformations to remove identifiable information from 300 TB of data, once per month to populate testing environments for building models

- Many e-commerce organizations these days work in a loosely coupled virtual fashion where various sub organizations work towards one common goal. For these organizations, speed is money — speed in the delivery of the goods to the customer is of paramount importance; speed to access and integrate multiple data sources on the fly to find out who their next customer is; speed to predict customer churn faster makes them succeed in a highly competitive landscape. Data Lake's Integration capability provides a precise answer to these types of e-commerce retailers and wholesalers, by enabling them to effectively pool together multiple unstructured sources with **Supply Chain Management (SCM)**, **Enterprise Resource Planning (ERP)**, and **Customer Relationship Management (CRM)**.

The following cases illustrate the practical scenarios:

- ° One of the US-based e-commerce companies use text analytics and natural language processing to integrate and transform 300 million unstructured medical documents each weekend into structured data that can be searched by users

- ° One of the Indian e-commerce giants reduced the development time by 70 percent by using integration and transformations written in MapReduce

- ° A Middle East-based retailer uses the Data Integration capability of Hadoop, to populate more than 250 data marts

The workings of Data Integration

The following figure depicts the steps involved in the Data Integration process:

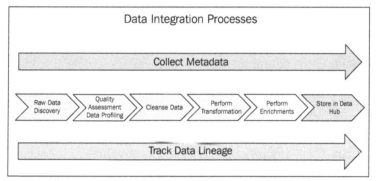

Data Integration flow

In the following subsections, let us understand each of the steps involved in Data Integration.

Raw data discovery

Raw data discovery is the first step to perform the Data Integration; this step involves finding out what data is available in the Raw Zone and selecting that particular subset of data used for integration.

The Raw Zone can be queried in its entirety or just the metadata can be queried to find out what data is available. For unstructured data, typically the metadata is queried.

The availability of data in the raw zone doesn't automatically entitle us to access it and conduct our favorite transformations on it. The Data Lake's security and governance mechanism ensures that we have the appropriate access privileges. More details on security and governance will be covered in *Chapter 5, Data Governance*.

After the data has been discovered for integration, it is accessed for quality compliance in the subsequent step.

Data quality assessment

In this step, the data is checked to understand how good it is; it helps in planning data cleansing and enrichment approaches.

Profiling the data

Data profiling is a step that performs a quick analysis to understand the suitability of data and then create a profile metadata about completeness, correctness, and coherence of the data.

The profile metadata contains qualitative information as follows:

- Metadata on how complete the data is:
    - Does the data have all the values to answer business questions?
    - Are there any missing values?
    - Are there any null-valued attributes?
    - Are there any unknown, nonrelevant values in the records?
    - In unstructured data, what are the important elements relevant for analytics?

- Metadata on how correct the data is with respect to the business context:
    - Are there any nonunique elements?
    - In unstructured data, are there strings with atypical string length?
    - For continuous values, are there any values below or above the minimum and maximum allowable limit?

- Metadata on how coherent the data is:
    - Is the data making sense relative to itself?
    - Does it have referential integrity across the tables?
    - Does it have value integrity across the values in a single table?

The profile metadata plays a key role in eventually improving the data quality by cleansing it. As it indicates what is right and what is wrong with the data, it helps the data scientists to take a calculated decision on whether to use the data or not to find analytical insights. In practice, this profile metadata is acquired across the complete data pipeline, including the Data Integration stage and various other stages during and after the transformation to help data lineage collection and tracking.

The following image captures the essence of profiling:

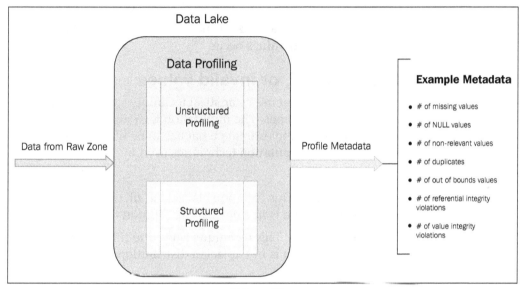

Data profiling

Data cleansing

Once we have a clear understanding of how good the data is through the profiling process, we now move on to ensure that the data is devoid of any quality issues as identified by the profile metadata.

In this stage, the data cleansing performs operations such as handling missing values, removal of outliers, handling null values, correcting invalid values, and so on. This will ensure that the inconsistencies in the data are removed well before it is used in any sort of transformations or analytics. The output of this stage is the cleansed data, along with the information on what operations have been performed on the data.

There are basically two methods to deal with this: one is to delete and another is to impute.

Deletion of missing, null, or invalid values

Once we have clearly identified the presence of the missing, null, or invalid values in the data, the Data Lake can use automated routines defined by a business to perform deletion. The deletion of data ensures that the data does not pass through the subsequent steps; the deleted data is maintained in a separate file to allow processes such as manual intervention and for audit purposes. The two ways to perform the deletion are as follows:

- Delete all records where missing, null, or invalid values occur
- Perform pair-wise deletion after analyzing the subcategories of data where missing, null, or invalid values occur

Imputation of missing, null, or invalid values

Imputation does not delete the data, but uses statistical techniques to fill missing, null, or invalid values with estimated ones. The imputation technique figures out known relationships in valid data, to estimate what has to be filled in for missing, null, or invalid values. Some of the imputation techniques used in data cleansing are as follows:

- **The mean value imputation**: This technique is used to fill missing, null, or invalid values when the data is in a normal distribution
- **The median value imputation**: This technique is used to fill missing, null, or invalid values when the data is in Laplacian distribution or when there are outliers present
- **The mode value imputation**: This technique is used to fill missing, null, or invalid values when the data contains qualitative attributes such as strings or characters
- **The prediction model imputation**: The Data Lake cleansing routines can use the prediction model imputation techniques such as decision trees, random forests, ANOVA, or logistic regression to predict and fill missing, null, or invalid values.

In a Data Lake environment, the presence of data from different External Data Sources adds its own complexity while cleansing. In order to deal with various sources and types of data, the Data Lake would benefit from implementing data cleansing processes that can deal with bad data originating due to:

- Erroneous ways of data gathering such as the manual entry of data fields, measurement errors, sensor calibration errors, and duplicate data from instruments.

- Flawed approaches of data delivery such as improper conversion, inappropriate joins, wrong handling of null values, and transmission problems such as buffer overflows.

- Inaccurate methods of data storage such as a rare problem originating in the physical storage (hard drives and archival storage) after storing data for a longer period of time within the Data Lake. This phenomenon is referred to as bit rot, which can be dealt by running specific routines such as checksums on the physical storage and replacing the bad blocks with good blocks.

- The invalid process of logical data storage such as the missing relationship between tables, invalid metadata, and wrong timestamps.

- Faulty ways of data integration such as performing joins using incorrect time synchronization techniques, varying field formats or schemas, or wrong choice of algorithms.

After the cleansing routines have done their job, the resultant dataset is evaluated to learn how accurate it is, and if there are any exceptions, they are corrected. Information about the data element that has been imputed and the success rate of the cleaning process is stored as a part of the metadata.

The following figure captures the important elements of data cleansing:

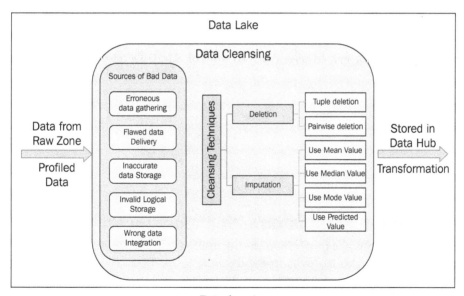

Data cleansing

Data transformations

In this stage, the cleansed data is transformed to generate better data for analytical purposes. It is an iterative process that has a considerable effect and it improves the accuracy and performance of the algorithms used to extract insights.

The following figure captures the important elements of data transformations:

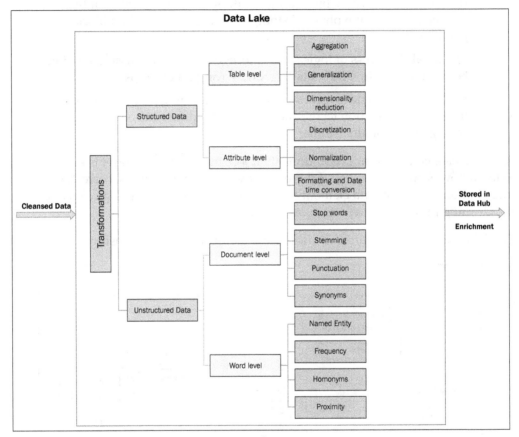

Data transformation

Unstructured text transformation techniques

These transformations are performed on the unstructured textual data at a document-level and a word-level. In the document-level transformations, the entire document's text is decomposed, transformed, and made suitable for further processing. At the word-level, each word entity is referenced for contextual relevance and the matched contextual information is stored and indexed for each word entity.

A few text transformation techniques that operate at the document-level are as follows:

- Word-level transformation techniques are as follows:
    - ° Named entity lookup and resolution techniques are used for extracting entities such as the name of a city, state, or country from documents
    - ° Frequency analysis and resolution techniques are used for understanding the number of times a given word occurs in a set of documents and then build a matrix of word frequencies
    - ° Proximity analysis techniques are used for understanding how many words occur together and how they are related to each other
    - ° Homonym extraction techniques to find how many words are pronounced and spelled in the same way and differ in meaning

- Document-level transformation techniques are as follows:
    - ° Removal of stop words from the entire document
    - ° Making documents case-insensitive or uniform case
    - ° Removal of punctuation
    - ° Stemming techniques that transform a word into its base form
    - ° Replacing synonyms
    - ° Replacing alternative spellings
    - ° Homograph resolution techniques in which abbreviations are expanded
    - ° Exclusion of negativity techniques deals with cases in which it is not necessary to parse or transform statements that have negative meanings

Structured data transformations

Structured data transformations are performed on the structured data. The two types of structured data transformations are as follows:

- **Attribute-level structured data transformations**: These transformations are performed on the structured data. A few attribute transformation techniques are as follows:
    - ° Binning is a technique used to discretize numerical attributes by grouping them into certain ranges. It is performed by dividing data into bins of equal depth or equal width. If the data is categorical, then the bins are grouped by each category.

- ° Scaling or normalization of data is performed to bring all the values of a numeric attribute into the same range such as 0 to 1. It also involves adjusting or fitting the data values measured on different scales to a notionally common range. This is done in order to remove the effect of very high values and very low values present in the data.

- ° Date-time conversion transformation is generally used to create a uniform representation of dates across all the integrated data.

- **Table-level structured data transformations**: These transformations are performed on the structured data. A few table-level transformation techniques are as follows:

  - ° The aggregation transformation is used to perform summary operations on the data, such as calculating yearly, monthly, and daily summaries from the data. It enables the creation of aggregates by joining more than one attribute into a single attribute and it helps to view the entire data in numerous dimensions and granularities.

  - ° The generalization transformation creates high-level summaries called conceptual hierarchies that group similar data with descriptive attributes that best describe a group. For instance, all people belonging to ages 11, 13, and 15 years can be termed as *teenagers*, and all those who belong to 20-22 age group can be termed as *adults*. These hierarchies can again be recursively grouped to form higher concepts until a certain level of descriptive detail has emerged. Generalization helps in reducing the overall data detail, but it enables an intuitive and consistent representation of complex data depicted in a meaningful manner. The various techniques such as histogram analysis, chi-square analysis, partitioning techniques, and so on, help to perform generalization.

- The dimensionality reduction transformation aims at reducing the number of attributes in the data without any drastic risk to the overall data integrity. Dimensions are reduced by analyzing which attributes can be removed based upon the need, strength, and relevance of the attribute. Techniques such as **Principal Component Analysis (PCA)**, wavelet transforms, **Support Vector Machine (SVM)**, Chi-squared test, information gain, and correlation coefficient scores can be used for dimensionality reduction.

Data enrichment

Data enrichment is the process of augmenting existing data with newer attributes that offer a tremendous improvement in getting analytical insights from it. Data enrichment often includes engineering the attributes to add additional data fields sourced from external data sources or derived from the existing attributes itself.

Enrichment offers a way to richly qualify an entity for further analysis and it has a phenomenal impact on the predictive model's accuracy. Analytic algorithms learn to build a model from a given dataset; enriching the data ensures the best possible representation of data to model a solution.

New attributes, which result after the enrichment process is done, are sometimes created manually or through automated scripts.

With structured data, it is often a result of aggregating or combining more than two attributes and decomposing or splitting them, to create new features. For unstructured data, enrichment is performed by extracting relevant text, performing named entity resolution, tagging the entities, and clustering entities into hierarchies.

The following figure illustrates various data enrichment techniques:

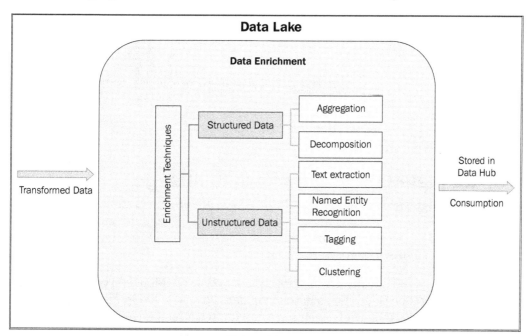

Data enrichment

Let us run through an example of enriching a person's address with the addition or integration of data from other sources. The original address data, the components of which are sourced from different sources, can be integrated with geographical, psychographic, and behavioral data derived from the address itself or other data sources.

The following figure depicts how address enhancement is performed and shows its benefits:

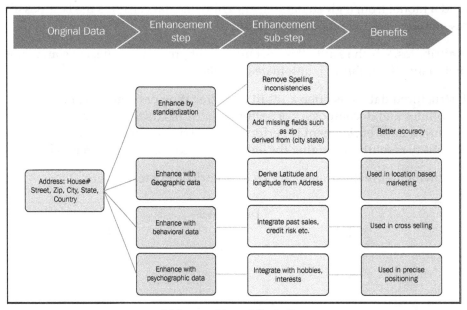

Address enrichment illustration

Collect metadata and track data lineage

As the data progresses through the multiple stages of data integration, metadata about the process and outcome of each of the stages is collected. Metadata is the heart of the Data Lake since much of the data discovery, provisioning, consumption, and eventual analytics depend on it.

Lineage tracking is essentially a Metadata-driven operation. Metadata collected at each of the data integration stages helps in tracking data lineage to aid in the understanding of the origins of the data and also helps in knowing what happened to the data in the past, when it passed through each of the stages of data integration. Data lineage tracking is usually performed by generating reports in graphical and tabular formats.

One of the fundamental benefits of tracking data lineage is to track data errors to the source by enabling activities such as data dependency analysis, error detection, compliance analysis, and so on. It also instills confidence into the customer about the integrity of the data being analyzed.

To enable robust data lineage tracking in the Data Lake, it is recommended, as a best practice, to build automated metadata acquisition and intelligent discovery from External Data Sources, while the data moves through the data integration stages. The Data Lake also benefits from an open-ended metadata repository that has interfaces to get, share, and enhance metadata from other tools and external customer sources. This metadata can also be synchronized across multiple instances of the data to maintain integrity.

Traditional Data Integration versus Data Lake

Traditional data warehouses integrate data, but they are not suitable for datasets that are often updated, resulting in the continuous execution of the extract, transform, and load processes for synchronization. Traditional Data Warehouses expose a query interface to aggregated and summarized data sources with no access to the original full data. This is a major problem when we want to integrate structured and unstructured data assets and build advanced predictive models.

The biggest advantage that the Data Lake's Integration capability provides over its traditional counterparts is that any data, whether it is structured or unstructured, can be integrated in its most granular individual transaction level rather than on an aggregate summary level.

Traditional data architectures are just no match for the Data Lake's horizontal scalability, which literally grows as the data volumes grow and scales up linearly as the performance requirements increase.

Additionally, the Data Lake's Integration capability enables minimal human intervention whenever there is a change in the hardware configuration of the Integration environment; the addition of new nodes to the environment doesn't really need any changes in the program that actually does the integration process.

The following subsections explain in detail how the Data Lake's Integration capability is different from a traditional integration capability.

Data pipelines

In this section, let us discuss how traditional data systems' data pipelines differ and how Data Lake addresses the shortcomings.

In traditional Data Integration systems, the following steps are generally performed sequentially:

1. Data is acquired from External Data Source systems.

2. Transformation and enrichment of the data.

3. Provisioning the data for consumption by down tier systems such as OLAP or SAS/R.

Each of these steps are performed individually and data is written into the physical storage before the next step in the sequence is started. This creates bottlenecks that can degrade integration performance as it uses an inordinate number of disk seeks and writes. This is one of the fundamental reasons why traditional integration systems cannot elegantly handle the challenge of Big Data. The following picture depicts the disk access pattern between each step:

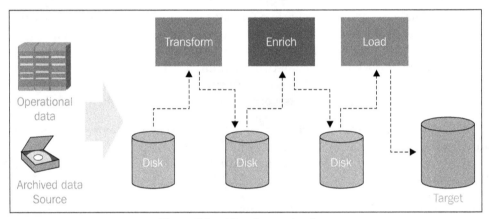

The traditional Data Integration flow

Addressing the limitations using Data Lake

Data Lake's reliance on the Hadoop platform for performing Data Integration tries to address the previously mentioned issues of disk I/O bottlenecks. Hadoop's inherent ability to build and model the flow of Data Integration processes using data pipelines addresses the shortcomings of the traditional systems.

Data pipelines are typically implemented by Spark that natively runs along with Hadoop Yarn. Spark uses a data flow paradigm that makes it intuitive for a lay user to build in-memory data pipelines. This data flow paradigm reduces the costly seeking, read and write to the physical storage to a certain extent.

Using this data flow paradigm, the data pipeline carries data from upstream systems directly to downstream applications whenever data is available and most importantly even before the upstream system completes processing. The following picture depicts the direct flow of data bypassing the disk access pattern of traditional systems:

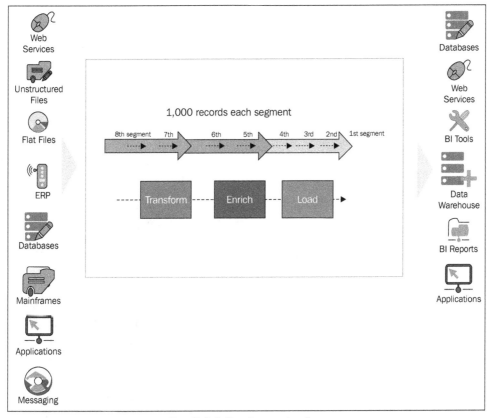

Data Lake's Data Integration flow

The Data Lake's Integration implementation using the data flow paradigm of Spark, does not use the physical disk as one of the intermediate hops to store the data temporarily. This is accomplished through the usage of shared memory constructs and pipes, buffering the data in blocks so that each execution step is not thrashing the system while executing. This enables the acceleration of the integration steps and allows concurrent processing by both up and downstream systems. Intuitively, you can think of pipelining as a method of horizontally sharing the load among the up and downstream systems.

The data flow paradigm uses built-in constructs that optimize or reduce the load distribution horizontally among resources so that multiple operations in the data flow sequence can be executed in parallel with multiple nodes. As a result of these built-in constructs, the developer or the administrator doesn't have to be bothered about managing the I/O processing between each step of the integration process.

Hence, owing to the preceding mentioned advantages, you can see why Hadoop-Spark-Yarn has become a tool of choice to implement Data Integration workloads, not only to crunch a variety of data effortlessly but also to integrate huge volumes of data without ever slowing down as the data size increases.

Data partitioning

In this section, let us discuss how traditional data systems' data partitioning differs and how Data Lake addresses the shortcomings.

Many traditional Data Integration systems lack the ability to automatically partition huge amounts of data so that it can be elegantly divided among the available resources, such as processor nodes. In this case, partitions are generally created manually for each data flow based on the available hardware configuration (a data flow can be thought as an extract, transform, and load step). The developer or the administrator has to manually assign physical partition boundaries for the data. Within each data flow step, the data is intermediately stored on a physical disk and the next step is manually started. This manual intervention is quite inefficient and results in time-consuming development and testing effort for rewriting whenever the data configuration/schema changes and whenever the hardware configuration changes.

Addressing the limitations using Data Lake

Data Lake addresses the preceding mentioned shortcomings of traditional Data Integration systems using an elegant method of dynamically partitioning data that is native to Hadoop.

Data Lake's data partitioning distributes the Data Integration process load vertically among the multiple nodes of the cluster and this distribution is performed by partitioning the data into various splits called **partitions**. Each of the partitions is assigned to a node in the cluster that performs a sequence of programming steps that aid in Data Integration.

As opposed to data pipelining, which is a horizontal load distribution approach, data partitioning can be intuitively thought of a vertical load distribution approach.

Data partitioning can typically be performed on data using a single variable as a partition key. For instance, we can consider the customer name as a partition key and split all the customers with their names starting with *A* to *F* as one partition and so on. The following figure depicts how data partitioning is implemented and how the load is split vertically using the customer name as the partition key:

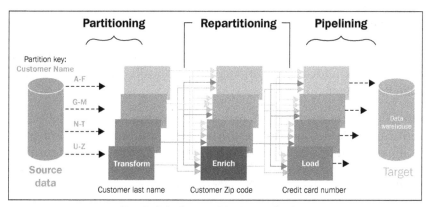

Data Lake's data partitioning mechanism

There are a wide range of data partitioning techniques that are implemented in Hadoop, which include the following:

- Key-value partitions
- Modulo partitions
- Range partitions
- Random partitions
- Round-robin partitions

All of these partitioning techniques balance and vertically distribute the data in such a way that every partition has approximately the same number of records. Using these partitioning mechanisms inbuilt in the Data Lake, the developer is not burdened with the nitty-gritty of manually partitioning the data, increasing the number of partitions, and repartitioning the data as a result of large amounts of data being ingested.

As you can understand from the above, the Data Integration framework of the Data Lake ensures that the integration process will be incredibly faster, less prone to frequent changes in configuration, require less disk management, and has less design complexity associated to cope with an increasing variety of data sources and business requirements.

Scale on demand

In this section, let us discuss how traditional data systems' Scale on demand differs and how Data Lake addresses the shortcomings.

Traditional Data Integration systems that are deployed in an in-house data centre do not scale gracefully to lodge data growth, as the volumes and data type complexity increases exponentially. They cannot adapt to the dynamic increase in the data load and they automatically load balance. Machines can be added to reduce the load, but they remain idle most of the time because there is no way that a complex integration data flow can be subdivided or partitioned automatically so that the newly added machine can be engaged.

The traditional Data Integration systems are not designed to comfortably coexist with various hardware architectures. In the traditional Data Integration approach, the applications developed on a particular hardware configuration cannot execute—without recompilation—on another large scalable cluster or **Massively Parallel Processing (MPP)** system that can handle large data volumes. This approach forces the developers and administrators to change the underlying code configuration because there is a change in hardware configurations as new hardware resources are added to handle Big Data. This shortcoming puts a scalability threshold above which the traditional systems cannot handle data volumes for integration.

Addressing the limitations using Data Lake

Data Lake addresses these constraints by providing the capability to follow a write-once-run-anywhere development paradigm. This paradigm ensures that you design, code, and test your Integration data flow only once. It abstracts the underlying hardware configuration details from the development process. Once the Integration data flow has been deployed, it can be seamlessly ported onto a grid compute environment with any number of nodes. The integration data flow doesn't have to be recompiled or reconfigured in cases where the compute environment is scaled up or down due to the demand that the data places.

This approach ensures that the Data Lake scores better in terms of overall Data Integration process execution time, as all the hardware resources are effectively utilized to crunch data. This approach also draws a clear boundary that demarcates hardware configuration's effect on the ability to run code, without recompiling or reconfiguring for every change in the hardware. Hence, this fundamental liberty to literally write-once-run-anywhere gives Data Lake the ability to provide scalability on-demand seamlessly.

Data ingest parallelism

In this section, let us discuss how traditional data systems' ingest parallelism differs and how Data Lake addresses the shortcomings.

As we have understood, Data Integration is all about accessing multiple data sources and combining them to generate better insights. The real benefits of parallelism cannot be realized even though organizations may have a Data Integration system that is built on a parallel RDMBS, until there is a way to ingest data into the integration workflow in parallel. This sequential data access from a single connection to the source system creates bottlenecks and bogs down the integration process considerably. This also affects the development time as developers and administrators have to manually handle the complexities associated with a single database connection and the partitioning of data.

Addressing the limitations using Data Lake

Data Lake uses Hadoop ecosystem's native support for parallel access to the leading databases such as Oracle, Microsoft SQL Server, Teradata, MySQL, and Netezza. Custom connectors can be implemented to support a variety of data extractions and storage from these databases in parallel. Data Lake facilitates the partitioning of the database while extracting the data from these databases and ingests into the Data Lake. This enables the Data Lake to access data from very large databases in parallel and integrate it efficiently by preventing any sequential bottlenecks.

Data Lake also provides the native ability to not only load the contents of the database, but also to read flat files in parallel. Files are partitioned using a configurable file pointer that reads an adjoining range or number of records from the file. Again, this ability of the Data Lake enables to integrate large volumes of flat files.

Extensibility

In this section, let us discuss how traditional data systems' extensibility differs and how Data Lake addresses the shortcomings.

Many times, we encounter the limitations where Traditional Data Integration systems are seemingly closed black boxes. Once a feature (such as sorting) is hardwired into the system, we have the flexibility to customize the way it performs to suit the ever-changing data needs.

In order to be really scalable and high-performance, these traditional systems lack the ability to natively support extensibility of features such as aggregating, sorting, and joins, and so on. There are cases in which a particular algorithm that is best suited for a type of data problem is written in another language such as C, C++, and Java. Traditional systems rarely possess the ability to parallely execute the code written in other languages.

Addressing the limitations using Data Lake

Data Lake possesses a unique strength in which Data Integration code written in other languages can be seamlessly integrated with the native code and executed in parallel. We can bring our specialized algorithm — for instance, one written in low-level C — and use the streaming capability of the Data Lake to integrate/execute in parallel along with the existing Integration and transformation routines.

Data Lake also has native support for executing the features in parallel such as aggregating, sorting, joins, and so on. Data Lake also supports run-time schema propagation, one of the key enabling factors for extensibility. Using run-time schema propagation, the Data Lake operates only on a specific attribute field/column of each record in the data, leaving other attributes untouched that are passed to the downstream system in the Integration data flow. This aspect enables existing applications to be integrated without making any changes, resulting in scalability and portability gains.

Big Data tools and technologies

Data Integration involves a number of sub processes that range from acquiring raw data to enriching the data before the data is used for consumption. There are many tools and technologies available that can sometimes be used independently or together to suit the specific business needs. These range from the packaged tools that natively operate on Big Data, to enabled technologies that let us develop tools that can work on our specific use case.

The following figure depicts the key aspects that are to be considered while choosing the right tools and technologies for Data Integration of structured data and unstructured data:

Structured Data	Unstructured Data

• Business Requirements
• Data Granularity
• Data Model
• Data Volume
• Data Complexity
• Data Latencies
• Real time Data Integration
  requirements
• Depth of Metadata
• Various Transformations
  required
• Data Security.
	• Unstructured Data
	  Acquisition
	• Unstructured Data Storage
	• Unstructured data
	  processing
	• Textual Classification
	• Ontology based entity
	  extraction
	• Volume of data
	• Contextual Mapping

The key considerations for choosing an Integration tool

Based on the preceding considerations and the associated trade-offs, you can choose a cloud-based Data Integration tool or an on-premise data Integration tool. The primary driver for making this choice is the cost associated for in-house deployment vs. pay-as-you-go benefits of SaaS models. Some Hybrid alternatives are also available, in which you convert unstructured text into structured data using in-house technologies and then use a cloud-based tool to perform the data integration along with report processing.

In the following sections, there are a few tools that are included here owing to their native support for the Data Lake's capabilities.

Syncsort

Syncsort is a tool natively implemented on Hadoop to provide high-performance bulk/batch data movement and integration.

Use case scenarios for Syncsort

The cases where we can use Syncsort for Data Integration in the Data Lake are as follows:

- To build native interfaces within the Data Lake Hadoop ecosystem to integrate internal and external structured and unstructured data assets.

- To write Hadoop jobs in the Data Lake to acquire, cleanse, integrate/ transform, and distribute data. It can perform almost all types of transformations on data.

- To seamlessly blend data from legacy systems, mainframes, and other No-SQL sources.

- To visually design transformations and optimize the execution on Data Lake's Hadoop infrastructure.

 More information on this product can be found at `http://www.syncsort.com/en/Products/BigData/DMXh8`.

Talend

The Talend Open Studio for Big Data integration tool is built on the Hadoop framework to provide an easy-to-use and intuitive Data Integration framework that can be leveraged by the Data Lake.

Use case scenarios for Talend

The cases where we can use Talend for Data Integration in the Data Lake are as follows:

- Talend is designed for ease of use and, hence, it is extremely useful for faster and easier drag and drop designing of transformations for data residing on the Data Lakes Hadoop infrastructure

- Talend's integration capability is enhanced by the fact that Talend has native connectivity with more than 800 connectors to acquire data from a variety of relational databases, flat files, and external applications

- Talend's data transformation and cleansing and profiling capabilities, such as anomaly detectors, formatters, and deanonymyzer, are the best of the breed and they are exposed as drag and drop components to ease the development lifecycles

- Talend can also be used to integrate with real-time and in-memory systems such as Spark

 More information on this product can be found at the following URL: `https://www.talend.com/products/big-data`

Pentaho

The Pentaho Data Integration tool gels well with the Hadoop framework to provide a visually appealing and intuitive data integration framework that can be leveraged by the Data Lake.

Use case scenarios for Pentaho

The cases where we can use Pentaho for Data Integration in the Data Lake are as follows:

- Pentaho has a rich GUI, with inbuilt visual components for integration jobs such as profiling, cleansing, and transformation. It can perform many standard types of transformations

- Pentaho has integrated parallel processing capability for a high-performance scalability

- Pentaho is designed natively to integrate with most of the Hadoop distributions such as MapR, Hortonworks, and Cloudera

- The administration and management of the Integration jobs is intuitive

 More information on this product can be found at the following URL: `http://www.pentaho.com/product/data-integration`

Summary

This chapter explained the Data Management Tier in detail; we started with understanding Data Integration and its prominent features. Practical Data Integration scenarios were explained to help you comprehend what Data Integration does in real-life scenarios.

The various steps involved in the Data Integration process were explained in detail; we then took a deep dive into how Data Lake excels in performing Data Integration when compared to its traditional counterparts. In the subsequent sections, we took a look at the various Big Data tools and technologies that can be used for performing Data Integration in order to help you in decision making and arrive at the set of technologies that can be used for specific use cases, by giving an overview of where these tools can be used.

In the next chapter, you will understand the Data Discovery and Provisioning Zones of the Data Consumption Tier; it will take you through the key functionalities of this zone and provide architectural guidance on how to go about implementing it.

4

Data Discovery and Consumption

In the previous chapters, we discussed the Data Intake and Data Management tiers. During intake, we have seen that the data is ingested from disparate sources and stored in the Raw Zone. The Data Management Tier performs data profiling and validation; integrates, cleanses, standardizes, and enriches the data and places it in the Data Hub Zone.

Let us now understand how this data can be discovered, packaged, and provisioned for it to be consumed by the downstream systems. Data Consumption comprises Data Discovery and Data Provisioning. In this chapter, we will enable you to understand the following topics:

- The process of enabling discovery in the Data Lake
- The various Data Discovery functionalities
- The important aspects of Data Provisioning such as data publication and subscription.
- The architectural guidance on choosing Big Data tools and technologies for Data Discovery and Data Provisioning

The following figure represents the end-state architecture of the Data Lake as discussed in *Chapter 1, The Need for Data Lake*. As shown in the figure, we will discuss the highlighted Data Consumption tier in the subsequent sections:

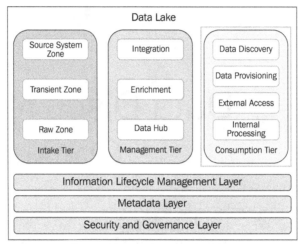

The Data Lake end-state architecture

Understanding the Data Consumption tier

Let us now understand the Data Consumption tier. We will start by taking a look at how the traditional approaches fail when dealing with Big Data discovery and consumption and how a Data Lake excels in this case. The subsequent sections will take you through Data Discovery and Data Provisioning in detail.

Data Consumption – Traditional versus Data Lake

The need for Data Consumption has grown more complex as enterprises are sitting on the vast reserves of potentially valuable but undiscovered data. With traditional EDW systems, the approach for finding data from disparate sources has largely been manual, inefficient, and time-consuming. The existing BI tools tried to address this by adding various data integration features, but they essentially provide visibility only into a miniscule portion of the data. The questions meant to explore the data have to be defined upfront; these models fall apart in the Big Data age where it is very difficult to ascertain all the intelligence that can be derived from a wide variety of data sources. With traditional approaches, there is no way of efficiently finding out and consuming the huge, high-value, multi-structured, real-time data assets that an enterprise holds.

Enterprises need access to massive volumes and a wide variety of multi-structured data to gain significant insights; we have seen that traditional models do not scale to address this need. There is a need for efficient ways to find the right data that is available from disparate sources to access, explore, and consume the data. The Data Lake eliminates the limitations of traditional approaches around data volume, variety, and velocity. It allows enterprises to bring all their data together and enable exploratory analysis of the data.

Data Lake exposes a queryable interface that allows self-service Data Consumption, where data consumers themselves can discover the data they need and request it to be provisioned. With Data Lake, data consumers can now go beyond canned reports and ask their own questions without the need for IT to build data models. This helps data consumers to discover and consume the data quickly and efficiently when performing data mining, business analytics, or advanced analytics on the data for their specific needs.

Multiple data requests such as raw data for statistical analysis or machine learning and transformed data for enterprise BI needs that can be serviced using the data available on the Raw and Data Hub Zones of the Data Lake, allow you to reuse data across the enterprise.

An introduction to Data Consumption

The value of the data on the Data Lake is realized when the data consumers can consume this data to derive insights from it. As we have seen in *Chapter 1*, *The Need for Data Lake*, the data is accessed from the Data Lake through the Consumption tier. The Consumption tier is governed by security, governance, and metadata layers.

Let us first understand the various actors in Data Consumption; they are listed as follows:

- A data owner: This is an entity who is responsible and accountable for the integrity, accuracy, and timeliness of the data. They help coordinate accountability by designating data stewards. The data owners are responsible for putting in place the controls for the collection, processing, generation, and disposal of data. In the context of data consumption, they define the security requirements of the data detailing the usage policies, classifying the data according to its sensitivity, and defining and authorizing roles that can access the data.

- A data steward: This is an entity who manages the data assets in an enterprise. A few responsibilities of a data steward are: creating business metadata by assigning a business meaning to data entities and defining data quality metrics within a business. In the context of Data Consumption, they monitor security, publish data, enforce compliance with the defined data usage and access policies that are determined through data governance.

- A data consumer: This is any entity such as a business user, repository, or an application that receives the data. This data can be used to perform further processing on it.

Data governance is a common process that is applied in the Data Consumption tier where roles, groups, and their privileges are defined by the data owners to restrict the unauthorized access to data. An efficient Data Consumption is facilitated by capturing metadata as the data flows through each tier. The metadata, thus, captured, can be used to keep track of all the data assets that are available on Data Lake. The following processes are applied on the data before it is made available for consumption in the Data Consumption tier:

- Maintaining a data catalog that describes the content, data definition, and all the metadata that is captured as the data moves in the data pipeline from data ingestion to data enrichment, integration, transformation, and consumption. The data catalog is published by the data steward to all the stakeholders.

- The data owners configure the security access requirements of the data, detailing who can access what data; the security details are stored as part of metadata, which is used by data stewards to enforce these policies.

- The data owners define the usage and access policies that are ensured by capturing logs to audit data usage, data access requests, and to monitor regulatory compliance.

These processes will be covered in detail in *Chapter 5, Data Governance*.

Data Consumption encompasses the volume, variety, and velocity of Big Data. The data can be consumed in a raw format from the Raw Zone or in a structured format from the Data Hub. Data Consumption comprises two steps, Data Discovery and Data Provisioning. These steps are performed on the data that is published. Data publication deals with making the data available for access. The *Data publication* and *Data subscription* sections discuss this in detail.

Data Discovery deals with searching and exploring the data to discover relationships and patterns and to identify relevant data through a queryable interface. Before requesting for the data to be provisioned, the data consumers would need to explore the data, with simple visualizations to determine the utility of the data for their purpose.

Data Provisioning allows data consumers to source the data available on the Data Lake. The following is the flow of events in the consumption tier:

- Data consumers initiate a search request through a queryable interface provided in the Data Discovery Zone.

- The Data Discovery Zone validates access to the data and uses the metadata and content indexes to identify the relevant data for the search request, and the results are sent to the consumer.

- The data consumer identifies the relevant data from the search result and sends a request for the data to be provisioned. The request for the data to be provisioned can also be initiated by subscribing to the data that is published.

- The Data Provisioning Zone verifies the security and access controls and provides the requested data to the consumer. There are various ways of provisioning the data; two of them are as follows:

    - Data consumers can initiate a secure pull request
    - The Data Lake can push the data into a predefined secure location

In the subsequent sections, we will discuss practical scenarios for Data Consumption and then focus on the Data Discovery and Data Provisioning components of Data Consumption.

Practical Data Consumption scenarios

Now that we have understood Data Consumption, in this section, let us get a feel of what Data Consumption does in real-life situations when specifically dealing with Big Data. Here is a compilation of a few cases:

- A SaaS monitoring organization ingests huge volumes of data such as time series and incident data from their clients' infrastructure, analyses it, and provides dashboards. They have historical data of over a hundred million records of incident data and incremental data of over three hundred thousand records flowing in. All the incident data is indexed and a queryable interface is exposed in the Data Discovery zone to provide a full-text search capability, in order to enable clients to efficiently search their historical data to identify what happened and fix the performance issues. The customers are now able to discover the data by querying using a specific term, view the search results using simple visualizations such as histograms, and are able to roll up the data to have a quick glance at the incidents. This provides real-time visibility into the events and actionable insights. The discovered data is requested to be provisioned to perform deep analytics on it in order to predict incidents and increase operational efficiency.

- With large-scale digitization, there is a significant growth of medical information; studies suggest that for every five years, the medical information volumes are doubled. Though this information is accessible, the consumers of this data such as practitioners have to browse, correlate, and relate multiple datasets to get relevant answers. A research organization collects all of this information and stores it in a Data Lake. Entity extraction techniques are applied to extract entities such as drugs, symptoms, side-effects, and so on. Relation extraction on medical entities is performed for extracting treatment relationships based on contextual clues using linguistic techniques. This data can be discovered where the relevant datasets are found and provisioned to apply further analytics on it to build question-answer systems that can provide precise answers to medical practitioners to help them in efficient treatment.

In the following sections, let us understand how use cases such as these are implemented in the Data Lake.

Data Discovery and metadata

Data Discovery deals with the identification of related data assets, making them discoverable and guiding the data consumers to relevant datasets.

The efficiency of Data Discovery depends upon the amount and quality of the metadata that is captured as the data moves across the various tiers in the Data Lake. Metadata keeps track of all the data assets that reside on a Data Lake; it helps data consumers to find the relevant data. Metadata identifies and maintains relationships between data, right from the time the data is ingested, enhanced, transformed, and evolved. It guides consumers to related datasets that can be combined and integrated.

Semantic metadata captures the semantics of the data; semantics is the ability to extract contextual meaning from text. Semantic metadata captures the context of the data and annotates the data with it; it can be used for data classification and identifying relationships between data. It improves search efficiency by providing a context for each dataset and visibility into the organization's data assets that reside on the Data Lake.

Data Discovery is a two-step process, the first step is making the data discoverable and the second step is performing the discovery. We will be discussing these two steps in detail in the following sections.

Enabling Data Discovery

The data consumers need to understand the data, its structure, content, and context in order to make efficient use of the data. Contextual information enhances the value gained, as domain data can be processed in conjunction with related datasets. Various techniques can be applied on the data in the Raw Zone and the Data Hub Zone to aid in identifying semantic metadata and to enable efficient Data Discovery. The following figure depicts a few of these processes:

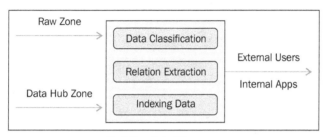

Enabling Data Discovery

The processes depicted in the preceding figure are applied on the data in the Raw and Data Hub zones to enable the discovery of the data from these zones. These processes are applied whenever new data arrives in these zones. As we have discussed in the preceding chapters, the Raw Zone is where raw data is stored; the original fidelity of the data is maintained in this zone and the data is retained here for active and archival use. The data that is cleansed, standardized, integrated, enriched, and transformed is stored on the Data Hub Zone.

Data is discovered from the Raw Zone when the data consumers need raw data with minimal enrichment to perform processing on it. The data from intermediate zones such as the integration and enrichment zones may not be required by the data consumers, as the Data Hub zone contains the data with all of these intermediate processes applied on it. Data Discovery from the Data Hub Zone is performed when the data consumers need to discover data that is cleansed, integrated, enriched, and transformed.

Data classification, relation extraction, and indexing data processes are executed sequentially. The following is the order of execution:

1. The first step is to classify the data to build and capture semantic metadata.
2. The relationships between the datasets are then identified by using the semantic metadata that is captured in the previous step.
3. Indexing of data and the semantic metadata is then performed to enable the discovery of relevant data.

Let us now understand each of these processes in detail.

Data classification

Data classification deals with volume and variety aspects of Big Data. Machine learning algorithms can be used to categorize massive volumes of multi-structured data into a set of categories or classes. We will now take a short tour of how data classification can be performed on multi-structured data.

Classifying unstructured data

Unstructured data is classified to derive semantic metadata by grouping and tagging it so that it can be discovered efficiently and quickly. The following figure provides you a quick snapshot of a few classification techniques that can be applied on unstructured data:

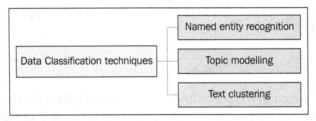

Data classification techniques for unstructured data

Named entity recognition

Named entity recognition is a subtask of information retrieval. Information retrieval is the process of extracting meaningful structured information from unstructured data. Named entity recognition detects and classifies entities based on the entity types they refer to.

Let us now understand how named entity recognition works.

Named entity recognition classifies the elements into a set of predefined entities such as organization, person, and location, and so on. It does not do string matching to classify entities, but takes the context into consideration to determine the correct entity type. It is a preprocessing step that is performed on the data before other processes such as identifying relationships are applied on it.

Consider the following sentence as an example:

Michael likes living in Washington.

The following entities can be identified using Named entity recognition:

Michael [Person] likes living in Washington [Location]

Now, let us see the implementation.

You can implement statistical modeling methods such as **Conditional Random Fields (CRF)**, **Hidden Markov Models (HMM)**, and **Maximum Entropy Markov Models (MEMM)** to perform named entity recognition on the data residing on the Raw Zone and the Data Hub Zone of the Data Lake.

Topic modeling

Topic models are a class of algorithms that discover hidden topics from a document corpus. They belong to unsupervised learning where one does not have prior knowledge of the contents of the document corpus.

Let us understand how topic models work.

Topic models derive connections between and within documents and take the context into consideration, which helps address synonymy and polysemy. Polysemy implies cases where the same word has multiple meanings; on the other hand, synonymy is about multiple words having the same meaning.

When a document is about a topic, we expect specific words to appear in the document. For example, if we are reading a document about medicine, we can intuitively assume that the words disease, patient, and diagnosis would occur frequently in the document. Topic Models work on this intuition; they examine the document corpus and discover topics based on the distribution of words and topics in the document.

Consider the following sentences as an example to understand how topic models work:

* My favorite colors are blue and green
* I met my friends, we all went to watch a movie
* A friend sent me a photograph of a colorful bird, it had hues of green, blue, and red

Applying Topic models automatically discovers topics from these sentences; the output might be as follows:

* Topic A: 30% colors, 15% blue, 15% green, ... (this topic can be interpreted to be about colors)
* Topic B: 20% friends, 20% movie, 15% watch, ... (this topic can be interpreted to be about movies)
* Sentence 1: 100% Topic A
* Sentence 2: 100% Topic B
* Sentence 3: 80% Topic A and 20% Topic B

You can implement topic models by using algorithms such as **Latent Dirichlet Allocation** (**LDA**) and **Hierarchical Dirichlet Process** (**HDP**) on the data residing in the Raw Zone and the Data Hub Zone of the Data Lake

Text clustering

Clustering is a technique that can be used to group similar objects together into a cluster, such that objects in a group are similar to each other and are dissimilar to the objects in another group.

We will now go ahead and understand how clustering works.

Clustering organizes a huge number of documents into sets of ordered clusters. When a corpus of documents is clustered, the search space gets divided and the search is performed on the cluster containing relevant documents. Clustering is an iterative process where the model is usually refined until the desired result is achieved.

Consider the following example to intuitively understand clustering. A library generally has various categories of books such as fiction, non-fiction, computer programming, and so on. Books that are similar are generally placed in one rack and labeled accordingly. Generally, all computer programming books are kept in one rack, all fiction books are placed together in another rack, and so on. When a reader needs a book that belongs to a specific category, he or she searches for that book in that specific rack instead of searching the entire library.

The implementation is discussed as follows:

You can implement clustering on the data residing on the Raw and Data Hub Zones by applying hierarchical algorithms such as agglomerative and divisive algorithms and also using distance-based portioning algorithms such as k-means and k-medoids. All these clustering techniques take text as inputs and convert the text into real-valued vectors by calculating the distance metrics.

Applications of data classification

The applications of Data Classification in a Data Lake are as follows:

- Extracting entities from unstructured text to build semantic metadata that can be used to identify relationships between entities and indexed to optimize Data Discovery. It enables extracting information of interest from a huge text corpus.

- Identifying latent topics from a document corpus; classifying and annotating the documents based on the topics. The latent topics, thus, identified are considered as the semantic metadata and eventually help in an efficient search and the retrieval of relevant data. It can also be used to summarize documents.

- Clustering search results to help in the efficient retrieval of relevant results, as the documents are organized into ordered groups; the classes can be used to annotate documents to enable access to relevant documents.

- Computing dynamic search facets in faceted search to enable exploratory searches and refine search results. The faceted search is covered in a separate section in this chapter.

Relation extraction

Relation extraction deals with detection and extraction of hidden semantic relationships between entities and data. The following figure depicts a few relation extraction methods for structured and unstructured data:

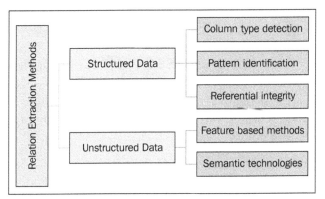

Relation extraction methods

Let us now understand each of these methods in detail.

Extracting relationships from unstructured data

Relation extraction from unstructured data opens up opportunities for organizing and querying the data. It deals with mining properties that link entities and keywords contained in datasets.

Feature-based methods

Feature-based methods extract a feature vector from the data; semantic relationships between entities are identified using contextual cues in the text, and these relations are represented as a feature vector. A distance method or frequency measure is calculated to represent text as a feature vector.

A predefined relation can exist between two or more entities. A relationship existing between two entities is called a binary relationship; these can be represented as a triplet of subject, predicate, and object. If the relationship is between multiple entities, it is called a multi-way relationship. For example, the relationship "is a student of" is a binary relationship that exists between a student and a university.

Part of speech tagging is an important preprocessing step that can be used to extract relationships. It assigns tags such as nouns, adjectives, verbs, and so on, to each token. These tags can be used to extract relationships. The relationship between entities such as nouns is defined by verbs.

Consider the following sentence as an example: Michael lives in Washington.

The verb "lives" defines the relationship between the entities "Michael" and "Washington".

Understanding how feature-based methods work

A feature set contains syntactic and semantic features from data. Syntactic and semantic features can be extracted from the data when a predefined set of relation examples are provided. These features can be used to determine whether the entities present in a sentence are related.

Syntactic features that are extracted include the entities, part-of-speech tags of these entities, the sequence and number of words between entities, and the path in a parse tree that groups words in a sentence into noun, prepositional, and verb phrases.

Semantic features include a path between the entities in a dependency parse. A dependency parse tree links each word in a sentence into other words that are dependent on it.

Implementation

Feature-based methods use classification algorithms to identify the category to which a feature vector belongs to. You can implement feature-based methods for relation extraction by applying algorithms such as **Support Vector Machines** (**SVM**) and bootstrapping on the data residing in the Raw Zone and the Data Hub Zone of the Data Lake.

Semantic technologies

Semantic technologies help in identifying relationships between data and standardizing the method of expressing relationships. It is a framework that links metadata across multiple datasets that are stored on the Data Lake. Semantic technologies can be used to improve the knowledge source visibility of the data on the Data Lake and greatly reduce the time needed to discover, integrate, and analyze the data.

Understanding how semantic technologies work

Ontologies form the core of semantic technologies; the concepts and relationships between entities that are used to represent a domain are defined using ontologies. They also define the structure of the domain, possible relationships and restrictions in a domain. Ontologies are used to share a common understanding on a specific subject area; they excel in cases where information from different sources has to be searched and merged. Ontologies can be used to provide semantic annotation, index documents, and data integration in cases where there is ambiguity in concepts and relationships in various datasets.

Let us examine a short use case of patient-oriented research to understand how ontologies can be used in real life. Ontologies can be used to represent the knowledge of the existing medical data that can be combined with knowledge from drug data and **Electronic Health Records (EHR)** to power clinical decision support systems that can help discover possible treatments and their side-effects.

Some of the semantic technologies are as follows:

- **Resource Description Framework (RDF)**: This is a representation of linked objects in a graph form; it can be used as a common data model and to annotate data. Consider the following sentence as an example:
  - ° Michael lives in Washington. This can be expressed as a triple of subject, predicate, and object—Michael [Subject] lives in [Predicate] Washington [Object].

- **Web Ontology Language (OWL)**: This is a language used to build ontologies. It is built on top of RDF. It adds additional constructs and shows how to capture subtleties of meaning. Like RDF, OWL is also expressed as triples; while RDF defines "How", OWL defines "What". It can also infer similar relationships expressed in different words to be the same. Consider the following example:
  - ° OWL can infer that if Mike is the brother of Joe, it also implies that Joe is the brother of Mike

- **SPARQL Protocol And RDF Query Language** (**SPARQL**): This is a query language based on RDF. It can query RDF databases to retrieve and perform operations on the data stored in RDF format.

- **Inference**: This is the process of discovering new relationships based on additional information or rule sets. This inferred relationship can be used to annotate the data. Consider the following sentences as an example:
  - ° Let us assume an RDF has the relationship: spinach is a green vegetable
  - ° An ontology defines that all green vegetables are good for health
  - ° The inference would be spinach is good for health

Implementation

You can implement relation extraction using the above listed semantic technologies on the Raw Zone and the Data Hub Zone of the Data Lake.

Extracting Relationships from structured data

Structured databases improve the accuracy of relation extraction as they hold known entities and their relationships. Unstructured data can be combined with structured data to extract entities that can be used to identify hidden relationships.

Relationship extraction can be applied on structured data by performing the following steps:

- The column type detection: The column type can be detected by accessing metadata (if any) or can be inferred by analyzing the values contained by the columns. The detection of column types can help in finding related columns.

- The pattern identification: Regular expression patterns are identified in the column values; these patterns can be used to derive relationships where two columns from different datasets contain values of a similar pattern.

- The referential integrity: This states the relationship between multiple entities in a relational database based on relationships such as the primary or foreign key. Identifying relationships in structured data relies on the referential integrity constraints that are defined during the design.

Applications of relation extraction

The following are the applications of relation extraction in a Data Lake:

- Map data consumers' unstructured natural language queries to a more structured format and to extract structured information from massive amounts of textual data for constructing knowledge bases.

- Enable data discovery where data consumers can locate and purpose the data according to their needs without the requirement for the data to be interpreted by data specialists. Provide the linkage between structured and unstructured datasets in the Data Lake.

- Enable contextual search on a huge corpus of data, sometimes using **Domain Specific Languages (DSL)**.

Indexing data

When dealing with unstructured data, indexing is the process of scanning a corpus and building a list of search words; it is a precursor to fast and efficient search. The words are assigned to the document they represent, and the efficiency of search depends on how well the assigned words represent the document content. Metadata and full-text indexing allows data to be organized based on its content for effective searching. The data in the Raw and Data Hub zones is indexed and ranked to make it searchable.

There are multiple ways in which indexing is performed and stored: inverted index, N-gram index, and document-term matrix are a few of them. N-gram is a sequence of n adjacent elements (these can be words, letters, and so on) from a given text. In N-gram-based search, the N-grams extracted from a text can be inserted in a vector space where they are compared to the other sequence of N-grams from search query. If vector representations of two texts are similar, then the two texts are likely to be similar.

The document-term matrix captures the frequency of words that occur in a document corpus. A row represents a document in the corpus and the columns are represented by words. This representation shows the words contained by each document and the frequency of those words. The document-term matrix can be used to identify the topic of the document based on the frequency of significant words in the document.

In this section, we will focus on inverted index.

Inverted index

Inverted index enables efficient and quick searching of text. It is a process of creating an index of all the words in a set of documents so that the words can be searched.

Understanding how inverted index works

The document is split into words referred to as terms. It extracts all the unique terms appearing in a document; for each of these unique terms, it maintains a collection of documents in which the term is present.

Consider the following sentences as an example, with each sentence representing a document:

- Charles Babbage invented the first mechanical computer
- Charles Babbage was a polymath

Before building an Inverted index, the text is preprocessed by performing the following steps:

- Converting all words into lower cases
- Removal of stop words
- Stemming the word to its root form

A sorted list of unique terms and their presence in each document is captured; an inverted index of the above two documents results in the following:

Term	Document 1	Document 2
babbage	X	X
charles	X	X
computer	X	
first	X	
invented	X	
polymath		X
mechanical	X	

Using inverted index, the search is efficient, as we know what words are part of each document. For example, if the search query is who invented the mechanical computer, the first document matches and can be returned as it is more relevant.

Implementation

You can implement indexing using the above listed methods on the Raw Zone and the Data Hub Zone of the Data Lake.

Applications of Indexing

The following are the applications of indexing in a Data Lake:

- Improved search and retrieval performance on unstructured data.
- The document-term matrix can be used by algorithms such as **Latent Semantic Analysis (LSA)** applied on this matrix, which can produce relevant results even when keywords do not match. A brief introduction to LSA is provided in a separate section of this chapter.

Performing Data Discovery

The data becomes searchable after the processes mentioned in *Enabling Data Discovery* are applied on the data. The next logical step is discovering the data; the Data Lake provides a queryable interface to search and discover data using the metadata or the data content. This interface provides a flexible, self-driven capability that enables the users to efficiently discover data and analyze relevant information.

The search can be performed on both the content of the file or the metadata, such as filename or file creation date; these can be used to query data. Internally, the Data Lake makes use of semantic metadata generated in the previous steps to give out the relevant results. The following sub-sections describe in detail the various Data Discovery functionalities that can be implemented in the Discovery Zone.

Semantic search

Semantic search retrieves meaningful search results for a search query; it does not search to find keywords, but is aimed at comprehending the intent of the search and looks for contextual clues of words available in the search space. It incorporates word variations, synonyms, and other elements of natural language to increase search accuracy. Semantic search infers the meaning by retrieving information from sources such as ontologies, RDFs, and XML. Adding a semantic search capability to a Data Lake allows data consumers to intuitively discover related data assets.

The following are a few ways of implementing semantic search functionality.

Word sense disambiguation

Word sense disambiguation is a technique that can be used when dealing with polysemy. For example, the word bank can imply a financial institution to save money or a river bank.

When disambiguation is applied in such cases, it picks the most probable meaning by taking into consideration the context in which the word bank is used. In our example, if the word bank is used in the context of saving of money, it can be inferred to be about a financial institution.

Latent Semantic Analysis

Latent Semantic Analysis (LSA) overcomes the problems of polysemy and synonymy by uncovering hidden semantic information from document corpus. LSA is a mathematical approach that does not have insight into the meaning of words; it uses word co-occurrence patterns to infer similarity. This is where LSA excels as it can be used to retrieve relevant documents of any language. Datasets that have multiple words in common are inferred to be semantically closer.

An LSA indexed database can be used to perform a semantic search. It does not do an exact match to return relevant returns; instead, it looks for semantic closeness between documents in a corpus by identifying co-occurrence patterns even if they do not share the specific keyword.

Faceted search

Faceted search enables data consumers to speedily locate the relevant search results; it performs dynamic clustering of search results that are grouped using the tags in the index.

The data consumers can drill into and explore the search results by selecting multiple filters. Whenever a consumer selects a value, the search results are reduced to display the artefacts that have that value. Further filtering narrows down the search.

For example, the search results of a query to find a book on Hadoop are grouped under the type Big Data.

The following are a few types of faceting that can be implemented:

- Faceting on field values, where the count of all the values of the field are returned

- Retrieving the count of datasets that were created in a specific range, such as dates

- Retrieving the count of datasets from the current search results that also fall under a given query

The display of search results is controlled through faceted search; this empowers the consumers to create their own navigation paths by drilling down and refining the search to find the relevant data.

Fuzzy search

Fuzzy search return search results based on a near match condition and not an exact match. Datasets that are likely to be relevant are located and retrieved using fuzzy search. This functionality is useful when querying in natural language, where there are misspellings or when the query string matches only a sub-string in the search space. The relevance of the result is sorted where exact matches appearing at the top of the list followed by relevant matches.

Fuzzy search is performed by using fuzzy matching algorithms; the following are a few of the ways in which fuzzy search can be implemented.

Edit distance

Edit distance is a way of identifying string similarity; it finds the string similarity by calculating the minimum number of operations that have to be performed on the query string to alter it so that it matches the string in the result. The operations can be any of the following:

- Insertion: Editing the query string and inserting a character; for example, if the intended string is "technology" and the query string given by the data consumer is "technoogy", editing it and inserting an "l" would ensure it matches the intended string. In this case, the edit distance is 1 as we made one insertion.

- Deletion: Editing the query string and deleting a character. In the above example, if the query string given by the data consumer is "technologgyy", editing it and deleting two characters such as "g" and "y" would ensure it matches the intended string. In this case, the edit distance is 2 as we made two deletions.

- Substitution: Editing the query string and substituting a character. In the above example, if the query string given by the data consumer were "technilohy", editing it and substituting two characters such as "i" with "o" and "h" with "g" would ensure it matches the intended string. In this case, the edit distance is 2 as we made two substitutions.

Levenshtein distance, **Longest Common Subsequence (LCS)**, and Hamming distance are a few of the measures that can be implemented to calculate edit distance. There are variations to the types of operations that are allowed by each of these measures. For example, LCS allows only inserts and deletions. Hamming distance can be applied on the string with the same length as it allows only character substitution. The unit of cost (edit distance) also varies for each measure.

Wildcard and regular expressions

Wildcard is a generic term that refers to a character that represents all possibilities. The character "*" represents multiple characters and the character "?" represents any one character.

Regular expressions can support wildcard matching. Search strings are specified as regular expressions to match a specific pattern; these search patterns are extremely powerful while performing string matching. They allow matching of the search string to any part of the intended string. This allows you to find relevant datasets that contain a specific pattern or datasets that contain a specific pattern as a filename.

Data Provisioning and metadata

The Data Lake provides easy accessibility to the data in its raw and transformed form; this increases data sharing across the organization where internal or external data consumers can make use of the data. The process of providing the data from the Data Lake to downstream systems is referred to as Data Provisioning; it provides data consumers with secure access to the data assets in the Data Lake and allows them to source this data. Data delivery, access, and egress are all synonyms of Data Provisioning and can be used in this context.

The metadata captured as the data, moves from ingestion through integration to consumption, is used by the data consumers to identify the origins of the data, the various transformations that were applied on it, and to understand the data structurally and semantically. Metadata in the Provisioning Zone is used to identify the data available for consumption, validity of access, subscription details of the data, the consumers who are authorized to access it, and so on; it captures the following details:

- Details of the data that has been identified for consumption, such as the version of the data, standard format in which the data will be provisioned, size of the data, message digest, and the number of records in the dataset for structured datasets

- Data catalog of the data being published and the details of the consumers that can access the data

- Subscription details of the data such as the subscriber or consumer details, the details of the data subscribed to, the format in which the data is requested for, and the time for which the subscription is active

- Audit log captures all the details of the data that was provisioned, the data consumer details, the time of provisioning the data, and so on

The Data Consumption tier ensures that the data is secured and entitled only to authenticated and authorized users. Before providing access to the data, authentication of the data consumer is performed, the authorization to access the datasets is verified, and appropriate security measures are implemented by determining role-based access to the data. Existing enterprise LDAP and authentication mechanisms can be leveraged to perform authentication, authorization, and to retrieve role details. The data owners define security and access restrictions of who can access what data from the Data Lake; authorization can be set at the domain level, file level, row level, or individual data element level.

Anonymization techniques such as data encryption, substitution, and randomization can be applied on the data to ensure data privacy in cases where personally identifiable information is present in the data or when the data is considered to be sensitive.

Data consumers can request for the data to be provisioned in the following ways:

- By subscribing to the data that is published
- Subscribing to the data that is discovered by the data consumers in a self-service mode via a queryable interface of the Data Lake

The following sections take you through data publication and subscription in detail.

Data publication

Data publication deals with making the data visible to the data consumers, allowing them to access, consume, and reuse the data; the metadata identified for publication is made available to the data consumers. As in Data Discovery, the access to data from Raw and Data Hub Zones is provided in Data Provisioning; the metadata available in the Raw Zone is published for data consumers who need access to raw data with minimal enrichment to perform processing on it. Metadata from the Data Hub Zone is published for data consumers who need access to data that is cleansed, enriched, integrated, and transformed. The data that has been identified for provisioning is placed in the Provisioning Zone for data consumers to access it.

The following operations are performed by data owners/stewards before making the data available for access:

- Identify the data that is made available to be provisioned
- If the data is sensitive, appropriate measures are put in place to ensure data privacy is not compromised
- Identify roles that can access the data
- Specify the time window for which the data would be available

The metadata, thus, captured is used to restrict access to the data where only specific roles can access the data or the data is available for consumption only during a time window.

Metadata can be used to specify the publications that need to be created. The data stewards publish the metadata containing the publication information; it can be exposed via a web interface, XML, or web services, and the data consumers can be notified whenever data arrives that is of interest to the consumer.

Data subscription

Data subscription is a request made by data consumers to receive the data from the Provisioning Zone; the consumers can subscribe to the data that is published or to the data that they have discovered via the queryable interface. The following functionalities can be made available to the data consumer during subscription:

- Browse the data catalog to see all the active data publications; the relevant data can be identified and a request to access the data can be initiated

- View all the data publications that the consumer is authorized to access and subscribe to the relevant raw data or integrated and transformed data

- Access all the personal subscription information

The data consumer can request for customizations on the data being provisioned such as the following; these are discussed in the coming sections:

- Customization of the format in which the data is provisioned

- Selection of specific data to be provisioned

- In case of a push-based approach, defining the target location where the data is to be provisioned

Data consumers can subscribe to the published data through an API, web service call, or through an interface. Active subscription details and consumer role information are captured in the metadata to verify the access information and the validity of subscription before the data is provisioned.

Data Provisioning functionalities

In this section, we will discuss the various functionalities that can be provided to the data consumers to consume the data as per their need. The following figure illustrates the functionalities:

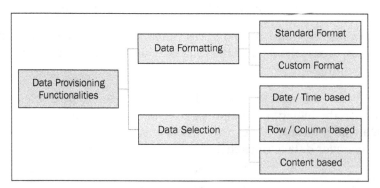

Data Provisioning functionalities

Data formatting

The metadata captures the format in which the data consumer requested for this data while subscribing for it. The Data Provisioning Zone uses this metadata to provision the data in the selected format. The Data Lake can support the following formats:

- Standard format: This is the default format in which the data is provisioned to the data consumer. The standard format is defined in the metadata while the data is being published; this format is consistent across the publications and is designed to cater to broader consumer needs. The data is provisioned in this format if the data consumer selects standard format while subscribing to the data.

- Custom format: The data consumer can be provided with an option to request for data to be provisioned in a specific format. Custom formats are generally specified in cases where the downstream system expects the data to be in a certain format. Without this capability, the consumer would have to reformat the provisioned data to meet the target specific format.

- While subscribing to the data, the data consumer defines the format such as flat files with a specific delimiter, the order of data elements, and fixed width data elements; all of this is captured in metadata and the file is provisioned accordingly.

Data selection

In most cases, the downstream systems would want to extract specific data or a subset to execute sophisticated analytics on it; the capability to select only a required subset of data can be provided using filters. The selections can include the following:

- Date or time-based selection: Segmentation of data can be done based on the date and time to allow data consumers to select specific data that was created or modified on a specific date or time.

- Row or column-based selection: This is applicable for structured data where the data consumers can select specific rows that match a condition or only a set of columns.

- Content-based selection: Data consumers can select the data that contains specific content such as any keywords that they might be interested in or the content belonging to a category or domain.

Data Provisioning approaches

The provisioning requests are served from the data on the Provisioning Zone. The full data or incremental data can be provisioned as per the data consumer's specification. The following are the ways in which data can be provisioned:

- Push-based approach: In a push-based transmission, the Data Lake initiates the file transfer of the subscribed files from the Provisioning Zone to a predefined secure location that is defined by the data consumer. The metadata information about the file size, checksum at the source, and other vital information can also be sent along with the file.

The target system to which data is provisioned can be a cloud-based storage such as an Amazon S3 bucket that can be accessed through S3 protocol or a secure location that can be accessed via standard protocols such as SFTP or SCP. The data can also be pushed to a messaging queue.

- Pull-based approach: In a pull-based mode, the data consumer connects to the Data Lake; once authorized, the consumer can pull the data from the Provisioning Zone. As in the push-based approach, the metadata information is also sent along with the file.

Post-provisioning processes

Now that the data is provisioned, a few processes are executed in the Provisioning Zone to ensure that the data transfer is verified and the provisioning activity is logged. A workflow can be defined to execute these processes after provisioning the data. The following figure depicts these processes:

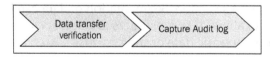

Processes performed after provisioning

Verification of data transfer is performed via acknowledgements through handshake mechanisms. The data integrity is verified as the last step in data transmission; it is done by using signatures, error detection code, and digests. If the transfer or data integrity verifications fail, the Data Lake can be configured to retry the data transfer for a predefined number of times or to send notifications to the stakeholders so that the transfer can be rescheduled.

An audit record is captured in the audit log for each push/pull request that is processed. It captures the complete metadata that was provisioned, the destination details, the status of provisioning, and so on. This can be used to keep a record of all the data that was provisioned and for audit purposes.

Architectural guidance

As evidenced in the previous sections, there are a plethora of options available for Data Consumption; choosing the right tool depends primarily on the use case you are attempting to implement using the Data Lake. We also see that the market is flooded with umpteen tools that make decision making very difficult.

Data Discovery

We have seen, in the previous sections, that Data Lake exposes a queryable interface to data consumers to discover the data. Simple visualizations such as a histogram or tag cloud can provide an intuitive understanding of the data. The following figure depicts the key aspects that are to be considered while choosing the right tools and technologies for Data Discovery:

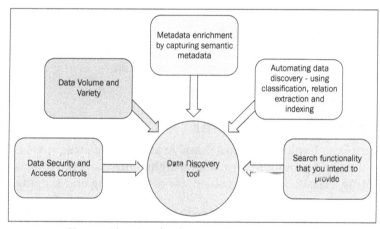

Key considerations for choosing a Data Discovery tool

Big Data tools and technologies

The following section takes you through an indicative list of Big Data tools and technologies that can be used for your specific use case.

Elasticsearch

Elasticsearch is a scalable search engine that provides a full-text search capability in near real-time; it internally uses Lucene that is a full-text search library. It searches the index instead of searching the text and, hence, provides fast search response. Elasticsearch provides plugin extension for indexing various file formats such as MS-Office, ODF, HTML, ePub, and so on. It uses Apache Tika to extract metadata and text from multiple file formats.

Use case scenarios for Elasticsearch

The following are the scenarios in which Elasticsearch can be used to discover data:

- Index metadata and the content of structured and unstructured data and to query them to allow relevant and fast search capabilities. It can also be used for language detection.

- Allow data consumers to search the entire data; Elasticsearch can be used to store the Data Catalog and provide features such as fuzzy match, autocomplete suggestions, regular expression querying, and so on.

- Elasticsearch can be used with Kibana to build custom dashboards to analyze, visualize data, and ask ad-hoc questions.

- It can be used along with Logstash to perform aggregations on the data to summarize it.

 More information on Elasticsearch can be found at the following URL: `https://www.elastic.co/guide/en/elasticsearch/reference/1.6/getting-started.html`

IBM InfoSphere Data Explorer

IBM InfoSphere Data Explorer indexes massive amounts of structured and unstructured data and provides contextual insights into the data. It uses analytics such as clustering, classification, and so on, for categorizing and tagging the data.

Use case scenarios for IBM InfoSphere Data Explorer

IBM InfoSphere Data Explorer can be used for Data Discovery in the following scenarios:

- Automate discovery of structured and unstructured data; it implements most of the processes that were discussed in the section, *Enabling Data Discovery*

- IBM InfoSphere Data Explorer can be used for federated Data Discovery and search

 More information on this product can be found at the following URL: `http://www-03.ibm.com/software/products/en/dataexplorer`

Tableau

Tableau is a tool that enables visual Data Discovery; it provides drag-n-drop interface for exploring data and provides visualizations to explore the data to find out outliers and trends from the data.

Use case scenarios for Tableau

Tableau can be used for Data Discovery in the following scenarios:

- Tableau can be connected to a Hadoop Data Lake to discover insights and analyze them in an easy-to-use, visual, and interactive way that helps business users to explore the data

- Data acquired from various sources such as social data, sensor, and clickstream data can be explored using Tableau

 More information on Tableau can be found at the following URL:
`http://www.tableau.com/solutions/data-discovery`

Splunk

Splunk collects and indexes machine-generated streaming data from multiple sources such as application or web servers, database systems, network traffic, and sensor-generated data in real time; it has the ability to connect to various data stores and enables the integration of machine data with the data existing in enterprises to gain insights.

Use case scenarios for Splunk

The following are the scenarios in which Splunk can be used for discovering data:

- Indexing machine data and logs and to add contextual meaning by identifying and tagging the data fields

- Automatically discover relationships in data and to provide visualization capabilities

 More information on Splunk can be found at the following URL:
`http://www.splunk.com/en_us/products/splunk-enterprise.html`

Data Provisioning

Data can be provisioned from the Data Lake by using native Hadoop file system commands to copy data onto a local disk. The data, thus, copied can be transferred to a destination location by using protocols such as SCP, SFTP, HTTPS, and S3.

For structured data, Sqoop can be used to provision the data from the Data Lake to a relational database. WebHDFS is another alternative for initiating a request to pull structured or unstructured files from the Data Lake to a specific destination. We have already seen the utility of these tools in *Chapter 2, Data Intake*.

Big Data tools and technologies

Apart from the above-mentioned tools, we will take you through a tool that can be used for provisioning data.

Data Dispatch

Pivotal Data Dispatch provides on-demand, secure, and self-service data access to the data consumers.

Use case scenarios for Data Dispatch

Data Dispatch can be used for Data Provisioning in the following scenarios:

- Data Dispatch can be connected to a Hadoop Data Lake for data consumers to discover and select data; access is governed by metadata and security layers

- Multi-structured data that is acquired from various sources can be explored using this product

 More information on Data Dispatch can be found at the following URL: `https://www.crunchbase.com/product/pivotal-data-dispatch`

Summary

This chapter explained the Data Consumption tier and we discussed in detail the Data Discovery and Data Provisioning zones of the Data Consumption tier. We started with understanding the various processes such as data classification, relation extraction, and indexing the data, that can be applied on the Raw and Data Hub zones of the Data Lake to enable discovery of the data. After the Data Discovery is enabled, we understood the key functionalities that can be implemented to perform Data Discovery.

We have also discussed Data Provisioning in detail, understanding the various functionalities that can be provided to data consumers while requesting for data to be provisioned. In the subsequent sections, we took a look at the various Big Data tools and technologies that can be used to perform Data Discovery and Data Provisioning to help you in decision making and arrive at the set of technologies that can be used for specific use cases, by giving an overview of where these tools can be used.

In the next chapter, you will understand the importance of Data Governance disciplines in building a Data Lake. It will focus on the common processes that are applied on the data as it passes through the various tiers such as intake, management, and consumption.

5

Data Governance

In the preceding chapter, you understood the various aspects of Data Consumption in detail, such as Data Discovery and Data Provisioning. We also understood architectural guidance on choosing the Big Data tools and technologies that can be used for Data Discovery and Data Provisioning.

In this chapter, you will understand the details of Data Governance; the following topics will be covered:

- Learn how to deal with management, usability, security, integrity, and the availability of the data in Data Lake
- Dive deep into the various Data Governance disciplines such as metadata management, lineage tracking, and data lifecycle management that are commonly applied on the data as it flows through each tier of Data Lake
- Explore how the current Data Lake could evolve in a futuristic setting

The following figure represents the end-state architecture of the Data Lake as discussed in *Chapter 1, The Need for Data Lake*. As shown in the following figure, we will discuss the highlighted layers that deal with Information Lifecycle Management, metadata, and Data Security and Data Governance in the subsequent sections:

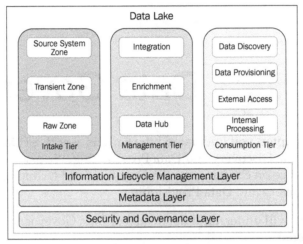

Data Lake end-state architecture

Understanding Data Governance

Let us now understand the definition of Data Governance; how it is critical in an enterprise handling Big Data and how it is different from traditional approaches.

Introduction to Data Governance

Data Governance is a set of formal processes that ensure that data within the enterprise meets the following expectations:

- It is acquired from reliable sources
- It meets predefined quality standards
- It is fit for use for further processing
- It conforms to well-defined business rules
- It is defined and modified by the right person.
- It follows a well-documented change control process
- It is aligned to the organizational strategy
- Its trustworthiness remains intact while data flows through various transformation cycles

As we can see from the preceding definition, Data Governance can be simply thought of as a discipline that an organization enforces on data as it flows from ingest to exhaust, making sure that it is not tampered in any way that is risky.

Data Governance is a key driver that is required to answer what an organization wants to achieve through its mission. In order to achieve its strategic goals, such as what markets to reach and which customers to serve, an organization has to create/acquire/capture data and convert it into intelligence quickly and accurately.

Data Governance includes the processes that govern the technology architecture dealing with data storage, acquisition, and management of huge volumes of structured and unstructured data. Once the data is stored, it has to be secured with the right information security policy applied to it. Data Governance deals with the security of the data as it is being acquired and as it flows through the enterprise.

As the data is searched, joined, and analyzed, it undergoes various transformations and is integrated with **Master Data Management** (**MDM**) systems to derive a new meaning; all the while, Data Governance processes ensure that the integrity and veracity of data is not tinkered in any way.

The Data Governance processes also help in the creation and population of a data catalog that describes the content, data definition, and all the metadata that is captured as the data moves in the data pipeline from data ingestion to data enrichment, integration, transformation, and consumption phase.

After the completion of analysis, the data that is past its use-by date is moved to tape storage or is defensibly destroyed so as to free up valuable storage space. This down-tiering movement and the defensible destruction of data is governed by Information Lifecycle Management policies that are in fact a subset of Data Governance processes.

The following figure captures the essence of Data Governance:

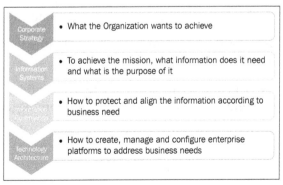

Data Governance

The need for Data Governance

The primary motivating factors for organizations to have Data Governance in place is to minimize information risk and maximize the value of information by extracting insights.

When enterprises do not follow well-documented and agreed-upon processes to access, use, manage, improve, monitor, and protect data, it is inevitable that the quality of analytics and decisions inferred from the data is jeopardized due to the inconsistencies that could arise from non-standard data handling. This exposes the organization to a substantial risk.

For organizations to comply with data privacy regulations such as HIPAA, Sarbanes-Oxley, Basel I, and Basel II, they have to invest considerable resources into the development of Data Governance processes that control their data assets and mitigate information risk.

Organizations following well-established Data Governance processes have systems in place in order to improve Data Security with fine-grained authentication and authorization controls in place that guard sensitive data from prying hands. Not only this, they have data leakage prevention systems to guard from data loss.

Data Governance also increases confidence and consistency in decision making since the organization is certain that the data is adhering to a verifiable quality regimen. This has a tremendous effect in increasing the eventual value of data, enabling optimal performance planning by data management staff and minimizing rework.

Governing Big Data in the Data Lake

The Data Lake addresses the storage, management, and analytical aspects associated with the three major facets of Big Data, namely velocity, volume, and variety. Governing these aspects of Big Data using the Data Lake involves adapting the existing governance processes to deal with Big Data and also to leave a margin of expansion for emerging trends in enterprise technologies and use cases of analytics.

The following list elucidates the Data Governance capabilities that ought to be implemented in the Data Lake to address Big Data:

- Classify data at field and source level in terms of confidentiality (for example, generally accessible, sensitive, and privileged).
- Classify data in terms of value (high value, medium value, and least value)
- Classify data in terms of retention schedule
- Govern various unstructured data types

- Administer streaming data and data sources

- Extract metadata from unstructured data and use it for classification and Information Lifecycle management processes

- Oversee access to Data Lake's analytical services (for example, by data source or data classification)

- Incorporate workflow management capabilities within the information governance solution

- Establish and control workflow processes for business rules

- Ability to request the resubmission of the previously submitted data and track status

- Ability to manage requests for elevated privileges for the users of Data Lake

- Manage requests for subscription to analytics artefacts

- Support an intuitive, wizard-driven graphical user interface for the administration of all information governance components and products

- Support version control for all information governance products

- Ensure the security, confidentiality, and integrity of data within information governance products

- Regulate access based on user roles

- Log and audit all information governance activity

- Document, in the form of manuals, guides, and specifications, all information governance processes and components

Data Governance – Traditional versus Data Lake

The need for effectively governing data has multiplied as enterprises are churning vast stores of unstructured, high-velocity, and potentially valuable but undiscovered data. With traditional governance mechanisms that deal specifically with slow-moving structured data stored in traditional databases, the approaches for governing data as it is acquired from disparate sources has largely been inefficient and time-consuming. With traditional approaches, there is no way of efficiently governing the huge, high-value, multi-structured, and real-time data assets an enterprise holds.

Traditional Data Governance mechanisms can hardly keep pace with the lack of structure in the data being captured. A few tools tried to address this by adding metadata capturing mechanisms to make sense of unstructured data, but they ended up providing visibility into only a small percentage of the data.

Traditional governance policies were in place to deal with slow-moving data that was acquired in batches in 24-hour windows. As the velocity of data increased, the acquisition window is compressed to a millisecond range, and hence there is a new necessity to change governance policies to define how this high-speed data has to be managed, how long it has to be stored, when it should be archived, and when it should be deleted defensibly.

Similarly, in the face of mushrooming volumes of data being captured, the traditional governance policies are inadequate most of the time to define the processes to be adhered to for Information Lifecycle Management. Various classes of new data would require changing the governance policies when it comes to classification of data and ensuring it meets quality standards. Organizations nowadays use massive volumes and a wide variety of data to gather analytical insights; the traditional governance models do not scale to address this need. There is a need for efficient ways to find the right governance process to acquire, explore, access, and consume Big Data. The Data Lake eliminates the limitations of traditional governance approaches around data volume, variety, and velocity, by bringing in all of the organization's data together.

Traditional Data Governance policies have little to ensure that the data acquired from third parties is indeed truthful. The veracity of data, when acquired from a multitude of sources (such as data from social media and other third-party data aggregators) other than your own enterprise, has a lot of questionable content; decisions inferred using this not-so-truthful data exposes the organization to a lot of credibility risk. In many Big Data analytics scenarios, it is common to use external third-party data along with the organization's internal data to infer valuable insights. The Data Governance policies that deal with Big Data would enable organizations to validate the truthfulness of the data acquired from third parties, before using it and eventually reducing the risk.

In the traditional governance scenario, it was easier to apply security policies on the data as it was more structured, slow-moving, and followed a well-set flow pattern across the various stages of the enterprise's data pipeline. In the Big Data case, it has become increasingly difficult to administer the security and privacy aspect of the data because of the sheer complexity of the types of data encountered, its velocity and volume. As some of this Big Data originates from third-party sources, it is very difficult to classify the eventual ownership of this data as public or private. Given these scenarios, traditional data governance policies should adapt to embrace the changing landscape of technologies and data analytics.

Traditional governance policies are in favor of defensible destruction of data, wherein data that is no longer valuable and not subject to regulatory retention should be purged from storage. This aspect runs contrary to the inherent promise of Big Data, which assumes that more data can be stored for a longer time to extract additional insights. Because there is new value in storing vast amount of historical data, there is a meaning in retaining data longer, counter to traditional defensible destruction policies. The Data Lake's governance mechanism balances the value versus risk aspect of data retention and destruction in a much better way.

Practical Data Governance scenarios

Now that we have understood Data Governance, let us get a feel of what Data Governance does in real-life situations when specifically dealing with Big Data. Here is a compilation of a few cases:

- A leading healthcare major followed Big Data-specific Data Governance processes to significantly increase its regulatory compliance score. It achieved this by ensuring that all aspects of data acquisition were governed by automating the acquisition of data from all sources, including internal memorandums, web page traffic and bulletins, and the careful distribution of that data to specific members of the staff who were authorized to view the data. This helped in streamlining the process and reducing the exposure to fines, compliance risks, and injunctions.

- A renowned aircraft manufacturer implemented a web portal that provided its entire staff vastly enhanced visibility into huge volumes of unstructured data relating to the various components for a new prestigious aircraft model under development. This visibility is made easy by the Big Data-specific data governance processes that help classify unstructured data to create structure around them and provide fine-grained access to the right staff. This automated classification helped enhance the speed with which staff were able to extract critical information from unstructured specification sheets, bills of material, and other PDFs. This eventually paved the way to avoid parts delivery delays and errors, which saved the company tons of money.

In the following sections, let us understand how use cases such as these are implemented using the Data Lake.

Data Governance components

Data Governance comprises of metadata management and lineage tracking, Data Security and privacy, and Information Lifecycle Management components. These are common components that cut across the Data Intake, management, and consumption tiers of the Data Lake. In the following sections, let us explore these components in detail.

Metadata management and lineage tracking

Big Data often relies on extracting value from huge volumes of unstructured data. The first thing we do after this data enters the Data Lake is classify it and "understand" it by extracting its metadata. Metadata is the fundamental building block, on which the success of any Data Governance endeavor depends.

Metadata captures vital information about the data as it enters the Data Lake and indexes this information while it is stored so that users can search for metadata before they access the data and perform any manipulation on it. Metadata capture is fundamental to make data more accessible and extract value from the Data Lake.

Metadata also provides vital information to the users of the Data Lake about the background and significance of the data in the Data Lake and helps in data classification using Taxonomies.

Taxonomies are relationships between data elements and are constructed by tagging data with information on how they are related to each other. The tagging of the data can be done manually by business users in cases where the business metadata of the data is known; it can also be done automatically by applying many clustering and classification techniques such as the *Topic modeling* technique that was discussed in *Chapter 4, Data Discovery and Consumption*. Taxonomies are implemented as parent-child hierarchies of relationships that use standard terminology to categorize data.

For instance, using the data contained in the rows and columns of a dataset, Taxonomy can be inferred about the columns' business definitions, meaning and its relationships with other business entities, and the various business definitions, classifications, and sensitivity tags associated with it. Using these inferences operational metadata, such as who can access, what can be accessed, and when it can be accessed, can be linked to the taxonomy.

This approach makes it possible to understand and relate vast amounts of data consistently just as similar as a taxonomy-based approach is used to classify billions of life forms into a manageable hierarchical structure of family-genus-species.

Once the data is deconstructed and classified, its other attributes are collected as a part of its metadata catalog. The following lists a general overview of these attributes, which are extracted and stored in a common metadata repository:

- Data identification information
- Data profile
- Data quality information
- Data lineage
- Stewardship information
- Versioning information
- Entity and attribute information
- Security attributes
- Data distribution attributes

Let us consider a quick example of sensor data to illustrate how metadata is collected in real time. There are different types of sensors that emit data streams such as weather sensors, water, gyroscopes, accelerometers, traffic sensors, and so on. They have different data formats based on the sensor type and almost all of them use hierarchical format such as XML. These sensors mostly produce real-time streams of data, except for a few sensors that transmit data at a defined interval of time.

For a supply chain organization that delivers goods to customers, weather sensors play a vital role in helping them to optimize warehouse stocks and delivery times based on the weather. These organizations typically get the weather data from the meteorology or weather station in the form of XML or RSS feeds and integrate it with their logistics data to figure out the best route to deliver goods.

Once the data is acquired from the weather station, it is deconstructed to extract the following metadata that would be part of the analytics:

Metadata	What is collected and derived as a part of metadata
Data identification information	File ID, timestamp, and a unique identifier
Data profile	Number of days of weather data in the file
	Number of valid temperatures
	Number of invalid values

Metadata	What is collected and derived as a part of metadata
Data quality information	Is the file type correct? Do the contents match the expected values? Does the file have complete data? Does the format comply to the expectation? Do the values of date-time and temperatures conform to valid ranges?
Data lineage	What is the source weather station of this file? Has the data or file undergone any preprocessing enroute? What was performed in the preprocessing steps? Was the data transformed in the preprocessing steps? Is the transformed data valid?
Versioning information	Specific versioning information for uniquely tracking and changing management
Entity and attribute information	Definition of all the entities and attributes such as: • Location • Station ID • Latitude • Longitude • Observation time • Temperature (both Fahrenheit and Celsius) • Wind (direction and speed in miles per hour)
Security attributes	Security classification id indicating whether this file is marked as public, private, confidential, or protected.
Data distribution attributes	User authentication information to access/modify/delete the contents of the file. Departmental distribution controls and access privileges.

The following image illustrates one possible view of how metadata is collected as the data passes through the various stages of the Data Lake:

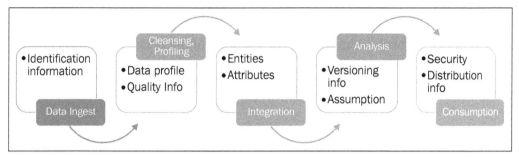

Metadata collection at various stages

The collection of metadata and the derivation of Taxonomies could be implemented in a distributed store to facilitate Data Governance. This enables the Data Lake to exchange metadata with other external systems it integrates with so that the data emanating from these systems could be traced as it enters the Data Lake. The mechanisms to index and sort the metadata store enable search, security, tracking, and transparent auditing of the data lineage when the data crosses into the Data Lake from external sources. This metadata-enabled data access helps in addressing complete Information Lifecycle Management issues right from data ingest to data disposition.

Data security and privacy

Data security is an integral part of the Data Governance process that ensures the data is confidential, has integrity, and is available at all times. Data security protects information from malicious and unauthorized disclosure, use, modification, and destruction.

Data privacy defines for what specific purposes data collected about individuals can be used, how long can it be retained and disposed, and respects the right of the individual to opt-in or opt-out from the data collection. This implies that the data in the Data Lake about any individual's preferences and tastes should be utilized only for the purpose specified explicitly; the data concerning individuals should be tagged with privacy metadata so that other processes may take notice. Privacy metadata can include sensitivity tags that identify an individual in the form of name, address, email, gender, national unique identifier, license, cell phone number, and so on. Marking personally identifiable data as sensitive is the first step in enabling the governance process to protect private data.

Security is a broad foundation that encompasses not only data but also its users, the processes that govern it, and the applications that generate it. Privacy is concerned with safeguarding the individual's information. Data can be secure without being private, but it cannot be private without being secure.

The following figure provides a quick overview about the policies that are enforced by security and privacy:

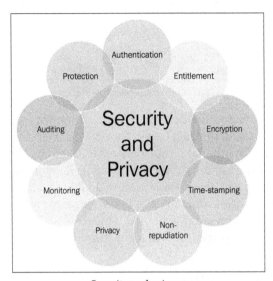

Security and privacy

Big Data implications for security and privacy

The data kept in the Data Lake poses a different challenge from the security and privacy perspective owing to its sheer size and variety. The following are the few important aspects of privacy and security of the data in the Data Lake:

- Greater volume of data kept in the Data Lake implies more surface area of risk in case of a data breach

- Newer types of data such as digital meters data, connected home data, fitness data, and telematics data have different privacy and risk implications than traditional forms of data

- The process of performing Data Integration, combination, and linkage with the sensitive data kept in the Data Lake can result in unmitigated exposure of private data

- A few of the datasets in the Data Lake are regularly used for experimental and exploratory analytics; this usage pattern can create unanticipated risk exposure to private data

- As there is a wide variety of unstructured data warehoused in the Data Lake, there is a high risk of exposure of data that is already under compliance regulations such as SOX, HIPAA, Basel, and PCI DSS

Security issues in the Data Lake tiers

Let us now understand the security and privacy concerns as data flows through the three tiers of the Data Lake as discussed in the following subsections.

The Intake Tier

The Intake Tier is the place where we interface the Data Lake with external systems and pull the raw data. One of the stated purposes of the Data Lake is to enable exploratory analytics on raw data, identify its hidden potential, and use raw data before further processing such as joining, refinement, cubing, matching, and so on. Raw data yields valid insights in many use cases such as entity analytics and fraud detection.

The data in this zone poses a high risk due to the following reasons:

- The raw data has not been "understood" from the perspective of usefulness; it is in its pristine raw state devoid of any classification about its eventual usage, authorizations, and privacy
- At the time of ingest, the raw data may contain personally identifiable information, and since it is untouched and no data masking has been performed yet, there is a higher propensity of exposing sensitive data
- Raw data containing sensitive information can be combined or linked with data already existing in the data lake resulting in security breaches
- Decisions and analytics based on bad raw data whose veracity or trust is at question can result in loss of face for the organization

The following are the few ways in which the security and privacy risks associated with raw data stored in the Intake Tier of the Data Lake can be mitigated:

- Perform raw data analysis in a quarantined landing zone where only a small number of authorized users are provided access to all the data
- Perform basic non-intrusive sanity tests to identify if the raw data being accessed is related to obvious business-sensitive information such as payroll, patents, and intellectual capital
- Use basic security controls such as user IDs, strong passwords, access control lists, and so on
- Encrypt file systems and monitor network activity across the intake tier to ensure minimal risk

The Management Tier

It is in the Management Tier of the Data Lake where the raw data is integrated with various existing data; it is profiled and validated by performing automated quality checks, and its integrity is established and eventually all of the raw data is standardized and cleansed into a well-defined structure that is amenable for consumption. It is in this tier that the majority of the metadata is collected at each step in the Management Tier. As the integration steps are being performed, the tracking information along with activity logging and quality monitoring information is stored in metadata that is persisted.

The overall security risk perception of data in this tier is relatively low compared to the Intake Tier, as the data is already parsed and deconstructed to identify the metadata.

The key to successful data security is to implement the metadata-driven governance approach in the Management Tier. The first step to use this metadata-based security approach is to classify or tag data based on different security and protection requirements of the multiple types of data deposited in the Data Lake.

In the Data Lake, not all data is born equal; some data is not worth the classification effort and may be deemed unimportant. Sensitive data can be classified by setting business-driven priorities and understanding whether the data is to be considered sensitive. If yes, is it based on personally identifiable information or corporate secrets? Data such as confidential design blueprints, internal algorithms, and its source code repositories are classified as corporate secrets. Once the sensitiveness of the data is ascertained, a business taxonomy is created to determine the relationship of the data to the users and applications that will eventually use it, paving the way for authorization and authentication controls built using this metadata. Using this methodology, the Data Lake tags instances such as customer payroll data, social security numbers, telephone numbers, and so on, as sensitive.

The Data Lake uses the sensitiveness metadata and the derived taxonomy to perform the following:

- Understand where the data originates from, by continuously monitoring external database access and file shares on the network.
- Identify on which component of the Data Lake the data exists now and how it relates to the other data in the organization.
- Help safeguard sensitive structured data contained in databases by preventing unauthorized access.

- Help safeguard sensitive unstructured data contained in the form of documents by redacting sensitive information while this unstructured data is being shared.

- Protect access to production and non-production environments such as development, training, testing, quality assurance, and staging environments by masking data that contains confidential information and keeps the functionality of these environments intact. Masking techniques substitute the real data with dummy data that looks almost real so that the data utility is preserved and the statistical integrity is intact for analytics.

- Safeguard sensitive production data by encrypting it so that it is scrambled and only the right user with authorization can see it. Generally, encryption is done on personally identifiable information so as to minimize the risk of security breach.

- Proactive monitoring of database and file systems that contain sensitive data to recognize any unauthorized data access and alert malicious access attempts, and thus ensure data integrity and compliance.

The Consumption Tier

The Consumption Tier is where the data is accessed and consumed either in raw format from the Raw Zone or in the structured format from the Data Hub. Data is provisioned through this tier for external access for analytics, visualization, or other application access through web services. The data is discovered by the data catalog published in the consumption zone and this actual data access is governed by security controls to limit unwarranted access.

In this tier, all the Big Data applications implemented in the Data Lake are integrated into the business workflow and are providing business value. This tier also works in a production mode where all the controls are in place and every data flow is regularly monitored for security breaches, regulatory compliance, and privacy audits.

In the Consumption Tier, the risk posed to data security is the least when compared to the other two tiers. As the security processes have already been operationalized, in this tier, we measure the effectiveness of the security processes against defined objectives. The effectiveness can be determined by metrics such as the number of monitored data elements that are sensitive, number of systems that are sensitive, total number of breaches, types of alerts, exceptions in file access patterns, data leakage statistics, and so on.

Information Lifecycle Management

Information Lifecycle Management is a sub-process of Data Governance; it is also known as Data Lifecycle Controls or Data Lifecycle Management.

Information Lifecycle Management is a process of controlling and managing the storage of data in the organization's infrastructure. The core idea of ILM is that the lifespan of data can be partitioned into multiple separate phases categorized by different patterns of usage and therefore during different phases, the data can be stored differently. ILM also helps to identify the true value of data over its lifetime and classifies it accordingly so that data is stored, migrated, or removed from the organization's storage infrastructure according to its value.

ILM works under the premise that the data has a finite lifecycle of relevance and the storage infrastructure has a finite capacity to hold data. ILM gives us a structured capability to classify data based upon business relevance by understanding how it evolves or grows over time, comprehends the usage pattern of the data, and eventually how it enables the organization to manage the growth in a systematic way so that the least business valued data is destroyed.

As data arrives into the organization, we can assume with a certain level of certainty that the data related to key business processes such as payroll, transaction processing, customer relationship management, and so on, does have an intrinsic value. Similarly, data in the form of generic email messages, memos, photographs, and so on, are relatively not so business critical.

As new data is acquired into the organization, the older data decreases in relative value; this can be ascertained by performing an analysis of the access pattern of the data. New data is accessed and updated often; as the data becomes old, its frequency of usage diminishes. The frequency of access is one of the methods to find whether the data is relevant to the business or not. There are other ways to classify data based on legal compliance requirements, privacy laws, data availability criteria, and eventual use for analytics, and so on.

The following figure provides a quick overview about the policies that are enforced by ILM:

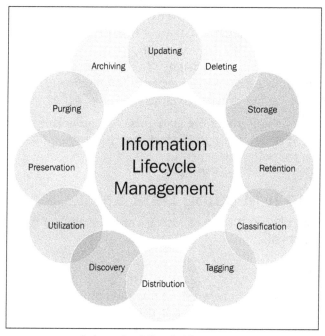

Information Lifecycle Management

Big Data implications for ILM

From an ILM viewpoint, Big Data is tricky to manage as a single unified resource across the organization. The following are the inherent challenges that Big Data poses to ILM:

- The more complex and varied the data is in the Data Lake, the more challenging it can be to govern and enforce lifecycle policies on it. There are data that come into the Data Lake once in a day batch update, and there are other data that flows in per second real-time update. The challenge is to neatly divide a combination of this data into categories based on their usage pattern.

- Newer types of unstructured data such as events, social, clickstream, sensors, and geospatial data stored in systems such as Hadoop; NoSQL databases pose their own challenges in terms of the veracity and eventual usability from an analytical insights perspective. Most of this type of data is not "generally" bound by legal, regulatory, and privacy norms. They are typically used in conjunction with the organization's own customer and financial or transaction data to produce insights. In these cases, there is not much need to apply stringent Information Governance Management Laws to these kinds of data sourced externally.

- The humongous volume of Big Data poses considerable challenges in enforcing ILM policies due to the fact that the volume itself offers a huge surface area for policy breaches and risks.

Implementing ILM using Data Lake

Let us now understand how ILM processes are applied as data moves through the three tiers of the Data Lake.

The Intake Tier

The Intake Tier is the place where we store raw data and enable exploratory analytics on raw data. This data stays there until it is used in any way. As the size of the raw data grows, most of the data would not have been touched in any way. This makes it complex to ascertain how useful the data is based on the data access frequency and whether to store the data forever in this tier or to move data into an archive.

The following are some of the mechanisms by which the ILM processes can be applied on the raw data in the Intake Tier:

- As the Data Lake stores unstructured raw data in file-based formats, data partitioning techniques give us the flexibility to classify it and govern it better

- In order to save considerable space in the raw zone, we could implement an automated process that can perform shallow compression on unstructured data after a configurable predetermined period of time

- We can implement columnar compression for structured data after a configurable predetermined period of time

The Management Tier

The management tier of the Data Lake integrates raw data and other existing data by standardizing into well-defined structures that is amenable for further processing. In this tier, the metadata is collected at each step of the process along with the tracking information, activity logging, and quality monitoring information.

In order to make real use of the ILM processes to govern the data stored in the management tier, the initial step would be to look at all the types of data that could be potentially kept in the Data Lake and perform a classification based on the following criteria:

- Which data is critical?
- Which zone of Data Lake does this data exist in now?
- How does this data flow within the Data Lake and how does it flow within the organization?
- What changes happen to the data over a period of time; will its value diminish? Is it okay to hold it in the Data Lake?
- The extent of the data protection and data availability needed for this data
- What are the business requirements of this data?
- What are the applicable legal policies?

Once all the preceding questions are answered we can classify the management tier's data into the following classes:

- Important
- Less important
- Archived
- Marked for deletion

The Management Tier implements two types of tiering techniques, storage tiering and compression tiering to store data. Tiering enables partitioning of data based on its lifecycle and class so that the least important data does not end up using costly storage; thus, improving the performance of data access and reducing overall costs.

Storage tiering allows data to be moved from one class of storage to another class in order to clear up space in costlier storage so that more important data can be stored in it.

Compression tiering allows you to use different types of compression to meet different access patterns of data so that the least important data can be compressed more since it is not used too often and it can relieve more storage space.

The following are a few suggested storage and compression tiers:

- **The high-performance tier**: It is in this tier that all the mission critical data that is frequently accessed and updated is stored. Here the level of compression used is negligible. This tier typically utilizes smaller and faster high performance storage devices such as SSDs. This tier is housed in the Data Lake's Data Hub Zone.

- **The low-cost storage tier**: This tier is where the less frequently accessed and relatively less useful data is stored. Here, the level of compression used is more. This tier is composed of larger and slower multi-array storage disks. This tier can be implemented in the Data Hub Zone as a low-cost storage array.

- **The online archive tier**: This tier is where all the data that is never used is stored. This tier is very large and usually stores the maximum quantity of data. Here, the level of compression used is the most. Typically, data is stored in an indexed compressed format so that it can be retrieved faster when necessary. This tier is located in an external archive database within the Data Lake; it uses ATA hard disks making retrieval easier than storing on tape storage.

- **The offline archive tier**: This tier is where the data that is never used is stored on tape storage. It is very similar to online archive, except that the tape storage is used instead of hard disks. One major disadvantage of tape storage is it makes it slow to retrieve data. This tier is optional to Data Lake and can be implemented when there is a need to offload the online archive.

If the data in the management tier does not fit in any of the preceding storage and compression tiers, it can be marked for permanent deletion. This aspect of ILM is called defensible disposition. The data is typically deleted in a manner that is defendable in a court so that the entire audit trails of the data from its creation to deletion exists. Defensible disposition of data is often mandated by legal and corporate policies, where it explicitly mentions the need to compulsorily store data for a certain time period after which the data can be deleted; this period is termed as Legal Retention Period. A few privacy laws in certain countries stipulate holding data only for the purpose specified, and delete data permanently to protect from the risk of privacy breaches.

The Consumption Tier

The Consumption Tier is where data is distributed in the raw format from the Raw Zone or in the structured format from the Data Hub. Data is consumed through this tier for external application access for analytics, visualization, or other application access through web services.

In this tier, all the Big Data applications implemented in the Data Lake are already integrated into the business workflow and are already providing business value. This tier implicitly assumes that all the controls are in place and every data flow is regularly monitored from the ILM perspective.

The following are the aspects tracked in the consumption tier as a part of ILM:

- **The distribution of Data**: As the Consumption Tier deals with the distribution of data from the Data Lake to internal and external data customers, every transaction that distributes data is tracked, logged, and monitored so that they adhere to the ILM policies of the organization.

- **The use of Data**: Once the data is distributed in the Consumption Tier, it is used by the data customers for generating analytical insights or for other purposes. ILM processes ensure that the right data is used by the right people by enforcing fine-grained access policies and also monitoring the usage patterns of the data.

Architectural guidance

As evidenced in the previous sections, there are a plethora of options available for data governance; choosing the right tool depends primarily on the use case and the level of governance you are attempting to implement. We also see that the market is flooded with umpteen numbers of tools that make decision making very difficult. The following figure depicts the key aspects that are to be considered while choosing the right tools and technologies for Data Governance:

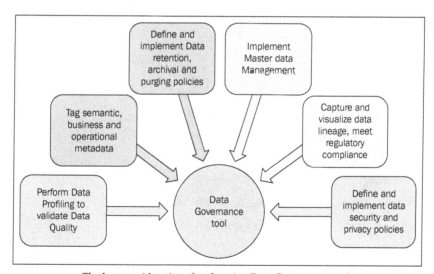

The key considerations for choosing Data Governance tools

Big Data tools and technologies

This section takes you through an indicative list of Big Data tools and technologies that can be used for your specific use case.

Apache Falcon

Falcon is a framework for data management; it simplifies creation, deployment, and monitoring of data pipelines. Falcon automates data ingestion, metadata tagging, and provides a foundation for ILM and governance capabilities.

Understanding how Falcon works

Falcon framework relies on three basic entities that are listed as follows:

- **Feed**: This is the dataset on which the processing is performed. Multiple configurations such as the cluster details and replication and retention policies can be defined for the feed.

- **Cluster**: This is the location where the feed is stored.

- **Process**: This is an entity that takes in the feed and applies processing logic on it. Internally, the orchestration is performed through Oozie workflow, and the process entity defines the workflow configuration to schedule the execution.

The preceding entities are defined independently using a CLI or REST API and are chained to build a data pipeline. It offers preconfigured customizable processes such as retry mechanisms, handling data that arrives late, policies for replication and retention. It also injects pre and post-processing steps into the workflows to manage the data pipelines.

Use case scenarios for Falcon

The following are the use cases for which Falcon can be used:

- Performing ILM by defining and managing data retention and archival policies for the data on the Data Lake

- Replicating data for disaster recovery

- Deidentifying personally identifiable information

- Orchestrating data processing through data pipelines

- Annotating the data with business metadata

- Tracking lineage and auditing

 More information on Falcon can be found at the following URL:
`http://falcon.apache.org/FalconDocumentation.html`

Apache Atlas

Atlas is an Apache incubator project that provides governance services on Hadoop to enable organizations to address compliance requirements across their data ecosystem. It maintains a common metadata store that enables sharing metadata within the Hadoop ecosystem and with other tools that interact with the Data Lake; this enables interoperability across multiple producers of metadata.

Understanding how Atlas works

At the core of Atlas is a type system that represents taxonomies and abstractions of the entities from which the data flows in; for example, a type can be a database or a table. Other examples of types can be the abstractions of components that Atlas interacts with; for example, spouts and bolts of Storm, messages and topics of Kafka, events, channels, and agents of Flume, and so on. The instances of types are the various attributes of types such as the data it holds, the storage descriptors, and so on.

These types are expressed as meta-models and are stored in a graph database repository. Atlas uses a graph database to store the entities, relationships between them, and the metadata; these relationships are used to classify the data.

The Atlas search interface provides a search DSL that is similar to SQL; it allows you to search through entities, lineage, and provenance. Search is powered by Solr/Elasticsearch. A bridge component imports the existing metadata from other systems; currently it supports Hive.

Use case scenarios for Atlas

The following are the use cases for which Atlas can be used:

- Securing PII data and protecting privacy and access using metadata-based access controls
- Performing ILM on the data right from its intake into the Data Lake until the time it can be archived or purged
- Defining or bringing in metadata information from other systems
- Classifying or annotating the data with relationships between datasets and data elements on the Data Lake
- Tracking and visualizing data lineage
- Capturing access information of the data for auditing purposes and enforcing relevant access controls such as time-based, location-based, and attribute-based access

- Using a text-based search capability on the Data Lake for Data exploration and discovery

 More information on Atlas can be found at the following URL:
`http://atlas.incubator.apache.org`

IBM Big Data platform

IBM Big Data platform allows governance of the data that is integrated from various sources.

Understanding how governance is provided in IBM Big Data platform

IBM Big Data platform uses the following IBM products for Data Governance:

- **IBM InfoSphere Information Server**: This supports capabilities to validate data quality and enrich and transform the data
- **IBM InfoSphere Data Replication**: This is used for replicating data across various data stores
- **IBM InfoSphere Federation Server**: This centralizes data access control and allows data access via a common interface
- **IBM InfoSphere Master Data Management**: This offers **Master Data Management (MDM)** capabilities
- **IBM InfoSphere Optim**: This monitors the data growth and ensures regulatory compliance by archiving data for compliance or purging the data based on rules defined by the business
- **IBM InfoSphere Guardium**: This monitors data access to ensure the security and privacy of data

Use case scenarios for IBM Big Data platform

The following are the use cases for which IBM Big Data platform can be used in the context of governance:

- Build metadata and store it in a common metadata repository
- Identify relationships between datasets in the Data Lake

- Define data quality metrics, validate the data against these, and perform predefined or custom data cleansing and enrichment

- Replicate data for high availability

- Implement security and access policies across the enterprise, centralize data access control, and provide access to the data through a common mechanism

- Secure sensitive data by masking it and capture audit logs to monitor data access

- Implement MDM throughout the enterprise and the ability to build an MDM registry

- Reduce storage costs by defining business rules around data archival and purging for performing ILM

 More information on IBM Big Data platform in the context of governance can be found at the following URL:

`http://www.ibm.com/software/products/en/infosphere-information-governance-catalog`

The current and future trends

In this section, let us explore where we stand and the current state of things with respect to the Data Lake and explore how the evolving enterprise landscape could potentially use Data Lake to enhance their competitiveness.

As I write this book, I evidenced that the usage of Data Lake was being adopted quickly. The know-how about new features, use cases, and new systems that are integrated with the Data Lake are being pushed into the public domain by a variety of industries and researchers at regular intervals. These developments would have tremendous impact on the way the architecture of the Data Lake evolves over time.

In the current scheme of things, Data Lake implementations across enterprises are dominated by Hadoop being predominantly used as a technology of choice for storing huge volumes of data and running algorithms in batch mode using the MapReduce paradigm. Hadoop has become a go-to tool for integrating and extracting better insights by combining unstructured data residing in Hadoop, with the existing enterprise data assets such as data in mainframes and data warehouses. Languages such as Pig, Java MapReduce, SQL variants, RHadoop, Apache Spark, and Python are being increasingly used for data munging, data integration, data cleansing, and running distributed analytics algorithms.

Data Lake and future enterprise trajectories

In the near future, we speculate that the organizations' data analytics strategies would evolve to provide the following capabilities:

- **The demand for extreme high-speed insights**: As the organizations compete using real insights, there would be a significant rise in the ability to capture data moving at high velocity, combine it with historical data, apply advanced analytics on it, and extract insights at a pace previously unthinkable. The Data Lake concept will be an ideal implementation strategy for organizations trying to analyze data moving at high speed by using architectural paradigms such as **Lambda Architecture (LA)**.

- **The growth of Internet of Things**: In the future, there will be an explosion in the number of businesses taking advantage of harnessing the data emanating from smart devices that are read, connected, and monitored in real time. Just monitoring these smart devices may not be sufficient; many businesses will mine for patterns and provide customers' usable insights. The Data Lake could help accelerate integrate to analytics cycle with smart devices. The Data Lake can also manage the data ingestion in real time and help find anomalies or outliers.

- **The adoption of cloud technologies**: There is an increasing trend in using cloud-based technologies that charge customers on a pay per use basis to use their storage infrastructure and their compute infrastructure to deploy applications. Enterprises will definitely take advantage of the capabilities built on cloud storage and compute infrastructure for providing Data Analytics as a Service and Machine Learning as a Service so that customers have the ultimate flexibility to use these services according to the workload. Implementing a multi-tenant Data Lake concept by the cloud providers can accelerate and optimize the provisioning of storage and compute environments that can process huge volumes of multi-structured data. Data Lake adoption on the cloud can be a valid use case, despite security being perceived as a challenge. The highly-secure and sophisticated infrastructure used in enterprise cloud services can mitigate security concerns to a great level.

- **The evolution of deep learning**: In the near future, organizations will compete to make sense of unmanageably large unstructured data and would increasingly apply emerging techniques that are collectively called deep learning methods. Deep learning methods are specifically designed to make sense of massive unstructured data and to find hidden patterns in it. It is an important tool in the Big Data scheme of things as most of the data is un-labeled and unclassified yet.

Deep learning is typically used to solve some of the intractable problems of Big Data as follows:

- ° Semantic indexing
- ° Classifying unlabeled text
- ° Data tagging
- ° Entity recognition and natural language processing
- ° Image classification and computer vision
- ° Fast information retrieval
- ° Speech recognition
- ° Simplifying discriminative tasks

Data Lake is poised to be the ideal paradigm to enable organizations to reap the real benefits of Deep Learning methods. The Data Lake stores data in a schema less representation, which is immensely useful for deep learning methods to extract complex, high-level hierarchical representations of unstructured data. Data Lake also enables to run complex deep learning algorithms on very high-dimensional and streaming data.

Future Data Lake technologies

We presume that in the near future, the technologies that go into building a Data Lake will undergo changes that can facilitate faster processing of data. As the cost per TB of data storage and high-performance RAM continues to drop, we foresee that there will be an increased movement of organizations towards adopting memory centric compute and analytics platforms that can harness the true power of in-memory processing for a faster turnaround. Data Lake architectures are bound to take a very good advantage of this drop in memory prices.

Data Lakes of the future can be built using both disk-based storage along with high-performance memory-centric frameworks. This will result in an efficient in-memory caching and data exchange layer that swaps data between disk and RAM based on work load and job priorities. This coexistence of two paradigms will be pluggable and scalable to enable the existing compute and storage paradigms to coexist together.

Newer technologies such as Spark and Tachyon are being promoted by UC Berkeley and Pivotal that are precisely implementing these concepts. Tachyon is the data caching and exchange layer that caches data from various data sources; it keeps track of the lineage of data and allows high-speed data exchange between disk and RAM.

Summary

This chapter explained in detail Data Governance and the ways to manage data with focus on its availability, usability, integrity, retention, and security. We started with understanding data governance and why it is needed and then understood how data governance on the Data Lake is far more efficient when compared to traditional governance. We also took a look at a few practical scenarios to comprehend the real-life use cases of Data Governance.

We took a deep dive into Data Governance and its components, such as data security and privacy, metadata management and lineage tracking, Information Lifecycle Management, and how they cut across all the three tiers of Data Lake, such as Data Intake, management, and consumption. In the subsequent sections, we took a look at the various Big Data tools and technologies that can be used to perform data governance to help you in decision making and to arrive at the set of technologies that can be used for specific use cases by giving an overview of where these tools can be used. We also understood the current state of Data Lake and mapped how it could transition to serve the emerging needs of future business cases of organizations.

This book explored the potential of Data Lakes and delved into architectural approaches to create Data Lakes that ingest, index, manage, and analyze massive amounts of data. We have comprehended the complete lifecycle of designing a Data Lake with the focus on the processes that can be implemented in the Data Lake tiers such as data intake, data management, data consumption, Data Governance, and the best practices that can be followed while building each of these tiers.

Index

About Packt Publishing

Packt, pronounced 'packed', published its first book, *Mastering phpMyAdmin for Effective MySQL Management*, in April 2004, and subsequently continued to specialize in publishing highly focused books on specific technologies and solutions.

Our books and publications share the experiences of your fellow IT professionals in adapting and customizing today's systems, applications, and frameworks. Our solution-based books give you the knowledge and power to customize the software and technologies you're using to get the job done. Packt books are more specific and less general than the IT books you have seen in the past. Our unique business model allows us to bring you more focused information, giving you more of what you need to know, and less of what you don't.

Packt is a modern yet unique publishing company that focuses on producing quality, cutting-edge books for communities of developers, administrators, and newbies alike. For more information, please visit our website at www.packtpub.com.

Writing for Packt

We welcome all inquiries from people who are interested in authoring. Book proposals should be sent to author@packtpub.com. If your book idea is still at an early stage and you would like to discuss it first before writing a formal book proposal, then please contact us; one of our commissioning editors will get in touch with you.

We're not just looking for published authors; if you have strong technical skills but no writing experience, our experienced editors can help you develop a writing career, or simply get some additional reward for your expertise.

Implementing Splunk

Second Edition

ISBN: 978-1-78439-160-7   Paperback: 506 pages

A comprehensive guide to help you transform Big Data into valuable business insights with Splunk 6.2

1. Learn to search, configure, and deploy Splunk on one or more machines.

2. Start working with Splunk fast, with a tested set of practical examples and useful advice.

3. Step-by-step instructions and examples with comprehensive coverage for Splunk veterans and newbies alike.

Scaling Big Data with Hadoop and Solr

Second Edition

ISBN: 978-1-78355-339-6   Paperback: 166 pages

Understand, design, build, and optimize your big data search engine with Hadoop and Apache Solr

1. Explore different approaches to making Solr work on big data ecosystems besides Apache Hadoop.

2. Improve search performance while working with big data.

3. A practical guide that covers interesting, real-life use cases for big data search along with sample code.

Please check **www.PacktPub.com** for information on our titles

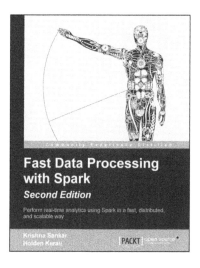

Fast Data Processing with Spark

Second Edition

ISBN: 978-1-78439-257-4   Paperback: 184 pages

Perform real-time analytics using Spark in a fast, distributed, and scalable way

1. Develop a machine learning system with Spark's MLlib and scalable algorithms.

2. Deploy Spark jobs to various clusters such as Mesos, EC2, Chef, YARN, EMR, and so on.

3. This is a step-by-step tutorial that unleashes the power of Spark and its latest features.

HDInsight Essentials

Second Edition

ISBN: 978-1-78439-942-9   Paperback: 178 pages

Learn how to build and deploy a modern big data architecture to empower your business

1. Learn how to quickly provision a Hadoop cluster using Windows Azure Cloud Services.

2. Build an end-to-end application for a big data problem using open source software.

3. Discover more about modern data architecture with this guide, to help you understand the transition from legacy relational Enterprise Data Warehouse.

Please check **www.PacktPub.com** for information on our titles